Contents

themes for early years

CD-ROM

- All songs sung with musical accompaniment
- All songs music-only version
- All rhymes spoken
- 18 photocopiable pages
- Ten full-colour photographs
- Five on-screen activities
- Three film clips

Introduction

Using themes in early years

Themes provide a useful way to link different learning opportunities. A theme on 'growing', for example, enables children to explore how to care for plants via practical activities such as planting seeds, making a hanging basket or growing beans. Themes can also help children to gain an awareness of the world in which they live. During the theme of 'growing', for instance, children will discover that plants need sunshine and water to grow healthy and strong, and that farmers and gardeners need good weather conditions for crops to grow successfully.

It is essential to choose themes that are appropriate to the children's knowledge, development and interest. As such, many of the activities in this book use natural materials that the children can collect or look out for as they walk to the park, the shops or their setting. Ongoing observations such as this will encourage the children to notice the minute daily changes of nature and to discover the natural life cycles of the world around them.

Exploring themes in the early years setting provides a wide range of opportunities for learning through play. In this book, for example, children are encouraged to use role play and dressing up during activities such as 'When I'm grown up' on page 19, they can find out how tadpoles turn into frogs while playing a life-cycle game, and will gain awareness of how plants grow by creating cress-head characters and by growing carrot top jungles.

A topic on 'growing' introduces many surprises, which will enable children to appreciate the delights of nature and the magic of creation. The theme also offers many opportunities for discovery and exploration, such as using the outdoor environment for planting, observing seasonal changes and investigating life cycles.

themes for early years

How to use this book

This book provides a wide variety of activities about growing, all of which link directly to selected Early Learning Goals and Stepping Stones as detailed in the *Curriculum guidance for the foundation stage* (QCA), and also selected play areas. The Planner on page 7 shows how these fit in with the six Areas of Learning.

Each chapter in the book presents different aspects of the theme of 'growing'. The first chapter gives the children a chance to consider issues such as growing up, and their future as adults. The second chapter covers life cycles and provides opportunities for the children to make comparisons between animals and their young. In chapter three, seeds and plants are investigated and ideas for growing real plants and flowers are provided.

Chapter four looks at how the growth of trees and flowers is dependent on the changing seasons and chapter five takes a look at how basic foods, such as fruit and vegetables, are grown. The final activity chapter highlights the variety of everyday things that come from growing plants, and reinforces the importance of recycling. Useful photocopiable pages relating to the activities are included throughout these chapters.

Four different display ideas can be found in the Displays section, all of which are constructed using the children's own work. These aim to help develop their interest and enthusiasm for the theme using creative skills such as 2D and 3D collage, painting, labelling and observational drawing.

The resources section provides a variety of songs and rhymes based on the theme of 'growing'. Each photocopiable page, song and rhyme is linked to an activity idea and can also be found on the CD-ROM.

Match the baby animal with its parent.

What's on the CD-ROM?

The CD-ROM with this book contains ten photographs, three film clips and five on-screen activities, all of which relate directly to the theme of 'growing'. The ten photographs include: a young baby, adults in work clothes, a colourful butterfly, a fully grown frog, sunflowers growing tall, leaves with veins clearly visible, a tree in four seasons, flowers growing in the wild, an allotment and a selection of freshly grown herbs.

The three film clips use fascinating 'time-lapsed' images to show different forms of growth in progress, for example, roots growing down, shoots growing up, and a spider making a web. The on-screen activities aim to challenge the children's skills and imagination by involving them in tasks such as dressing a family of bears, manoeuvring jigsaw pieces, sequencing plant pictures according to stages of growth, counting rings on tree stumps and designing an imaginary flower. The children will also be able to enjoy listening to, and joining in with, audio versions of the songs and rhymes highlighted in the resources section.

Planner

Use this guide to link the activity ideas into your planning for the six Areas of Learning.

Growing

themes for early years

Assessment

Assessment can help establish a clear understanding of each child's skills, knowledge and progress in all six Areas of Learning, and can be used to ensure effective coverage of the curriculum. Use a mixture of different approaches and ensure that these are ongoing, noting down observations as soon as possible, gathering information regularly and always keeping your records up to date. The children being assessed should be in familiar surroundings and engaged in activities that they enjoy.

Opportunities for assessment

Every activity in this book has an Assessment section which provides an indication of what to look out for when observing the children perform the task. These suggestions focus on identifying the children's willingness to explore, their ability to ask and answer questions and their enthusiasm for making comments.

Use a range of procedures to assess the children, for example:

- **Talking, listening and asking questions**

Gain an awareness of what the children know, recall and understand by asking open questions, using terms such as, *how, why, when* and *where*, to help stimulate responses. The information gathered could then be used to identify areas where individual children might need support or extension activities. Opportunities for informal assessment within this book include, the 'Body building' game, page 16, and the activity titled 'Baby clothes', page 9, which can be used to help assess the children's mathematical language. All the CD-ROM on-screen activities can be used to help assess the children's communication and descriptive skills.

- **Joining in with play sessions**

The practitioner can gain an extra insight into each child's use of language, their vocabulary and comprehension by playing alongside them. Take notes after the session and use these to help support short-term planning and to provide up-to-date information for other practitioners, parents and carers. The games titled 'Who's my mother?' on page 22 and 'Veggie snap' on page 57 both offer a practical opportunity for assessment, and a wealth of information can be gathered by joining in with the children as they view the CD-ROM film clips.

- **Collecting samples of achievement**

Collect samples of the children's handwriting, number work and drawings and photograph a selection of their models and constructions. Over time, the materials gathered will constitute an informative and practical record of each child's progress and achievements. 'Playing the game', page 69 and 'Growing roots', page 41, can be used to record pencil control; 'The cracking egg', page 31, and the 'Butterfly jigsaw', page 33 can be used to assess sequencing skills and practical activities such as 'Leaves have veins' on page 39, and 'Incy Wincy' on page 29 could be used to assess manipulative skills.

I'm growing up

This chapter covers the stages of human growth from birth through to old age, and invites the children to look at all the changes that will happen to them as they grow up.

STEPPING STONE
Say with confidence the number that is one more than a given number.

EARLY LEARNING GOAL
Find one more or less than a number from one to ten. (MD)

ASSESSMENT
Are the children beginning to gain an awareness of mathematical terms such as 'one more', 'one less', 'more than' and 'less than'?

Baby clothes

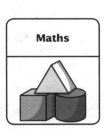

Maths

What you need
Five items of baby clothing (or five separate pictures showing baby clothes); a length of string secured safely between two points at the children's height; five pegs.

What to do
Sing this rhyme with the children to the tune of 'Five Currant Buns in a Baker's Shop'. As everyone sings, encourage one child at a time to collect an item of clothing off the 'washing line':

Five baby clothes on the washing line,
Drying in the wind and the warm sunshine,
Along comes (child's name) to feel if they are dry,
Takes a baby's (bib, hat, vest) and goes inside.
(Count down to 'no baby clothes', then sing)
No baby clothes on the washing line,
Nothing to dry in the warm sunshine,
Along comes (child's name) to hang up some more,
But oh dear me it's going to pour!

Discussion
Add and remove items from the washing line, asking questions such as: *How many clothes are on the line? Are there more than three yellow items on the line?* Talk with the children about what babies need, for example, bottles, bibs and nappies. How do these needs change as the baby grows up.

Follow-up activities
● Help each child to draw a 'washing line' across the top of a strip of card. Together, cut out pictures of baby clothes to attach to the line using Velcro tabs. Encourage the children to remove the pictures one at a time as they sing the song together.
● Invite the children to view the photograph of a baby on the CD-ROM. Ask them to name some clothes worn by babies, for example, bib, booties, romper, bonnet and so on.

Differentiation
Help younger or less able children to count the items left on the line after each verse. Older children could sing about ten items on the line.

ON THE CD-ROM
● Photograph of a baby.

Outdoor environment

themes for early years

Balancing act

STEPPING STONE
Combine and repeat a range of movements.

EARLY LEARNING GOAL
Travel around, under, over and through balancing and climbing equipment. (PD)

ASSESSMENT
Are the children keen to practise their balancing skills?

What you need
A large circular or wavy chalk mark on the ground outside; a long sturdy bench.

What to do
Encourage the children to move carefully along the chalk line in different ways, for example, walking, jumping, hopping, crouching down low, using giant steps or using tiny steps. Invite them to join in a game of Follow-my-leader by taking it in turns to be the 'leader'. Ask each 'leader' to move along the line using three different techniques for the rest of the group to copy. Challenge the children further by inviting them to keep their balance as they move in different ways along a study bench. Extend the activity further by using four benches to create a square for an adapted version of the Follow-my-leader game.

Discussion
Ask the children which way they found easiest to walk along the line. Did their outstretched arms help them to balance? Can anyone describe what happens when a baby tries to walk (wobbles, stumbles)? The children were toddlers once themselves and had to learn how to balance. Why is it easy for them to walk now? Do they know why a newly-born foal needs to find its balance very quickly? When a young bird is ready to leave the nest it takes little practice flights to learn how to balance when flying. Can they think of any people who are especially good at balancing (ballet dancers, gymnasts, ice skaters, skiers, footballers, horse riders)? Why do some older people use a walking stick?

Follow-up activities
- Cut up a copy of the photocopiable sheet 'Growing up' on page 11 for each child and ask them to arrange the pictures in age sequence.
- Invite the children to choose a friend to play with on the see-saw. Can they balance it in mid-air?
- Sing and play the 'Hokey Cokey' from *Oranges and Lemons* compiled by Karen King (Oxford University Press).
- Read the poem 'When I was a baby' on page 89.

Differentiation
Help younger or less able children to stretch their arms out at either side to help balance themselves. Encourage older or more able children to try walking sideways along the line or bench.

ON THE CD-ROM
- Photocopiable sheet 'Growing up'
- Poem 'When I was a baby'

Growing up

● Cut out the pictures. Put them into the correct order.

Construction and malleable materials

Happy birthday to you!

What you need

Clay; laminated or wooden board; jug of water; comb; pointed tool or pencil; cotton bud halves; paint and brushes; PVA glue.

What to do

Let the children enjoy playing with the clay by pulling, pinching and rolling it. If it starts to get too dry, wet it slightly with fingertips dipped in water. Tell them to roll it into a ball and then squash it flat with the palm of their hand. Use the comb or a pointed tool to mark indentations in the clay 'cake' for decoration.

Each child should count out the same number of cotton bud candles as their age and then stick them into the cake. Initial each child's cake on the base.

Leave the clay to dry for 24 hours. When the cakes are dry, let the children choose which colour they want to paint them. When the paint is thoroughly dry (not long because the clay is very absorbent) brush on a glaze of watered-down PVA glue. Don't worry if it looks white, it will be clear when it dries.

Sing 'Happy Birthday' to whoever is having a pretend birthday. Clap your hands and count for each candle that there is on the cake.

Discussion

Ask the children why we celebrate birthdays. Do they know when their birthday is and how old they will be on their next one? How old were they last year? In what ways can they tell they are growing older? Use the theme of candles to highlight important issues such as never playing with matches.

Follow-up activities
- Help the children to complete the sequencing activity on the photocopiable sheet 'Candles on a cake' on page 13.
- Have a pretend birthday party in the home corner.
- Play Pass the parcel with a surprise present hidden in the wrapping.
- Use a candle to make a wax resist picture.
- Read the poem 'Birthdays' on page 89.

Differentiation

Wrap up some presents and ask younger children to try to guess what they are from their shape. Cut a real cake into pieces and show older or more able children how to make halves, quarters and eighths.

STEPPING STONE
Show an interest in numbers and counting.

EARLY LEARNING GOAL
Use developing mathematical ideas and methods to solve practical problems. (MD)

ASSESSMENT
Can the children use mathematical ideas and methods to solve practical problems?

ON THE CD-ROM
- Photocopiable sheet 'Candles on a cake'
- Poem 'Birthdays'

Candles on a cake

themes for early years

STEPPING STONE
Initiate conversation, attend to and take account of what others say, and use talk to resolve disagreements.

EARLY LEARNING GOAL
Interact with others, negotiating plans and activities and taking turns in conversation. (CLL)

ASSESSMENT
Do the children join in discussion, initiate conversation and listen carefully to others as they construct and play?

Different sizes

What you need
A copy of the photocopiable sheet 'Growing bigger' on page 15; scissors; coloured pens.

What to do
Provide the children with an A4 or A3 card copy of the photocopiable sheet 'Growing bigger'. Help them to construct a set of eight playing cards by colouring in and cutting out the pictures showing four teddy tops and four teddy trousers. Encourage the children to sort and match the eight pictures to create a set of four teddies in four different sizes. Ask the children to place the four teddy pictures in order of size and ask questions such as: *Which teddy is the smallest? Which teddy is the biggest? Can you find two teddies bigger than this one? How many teddies are smaller than the teddy wearing green trousers?*

Discussion
Use the pictures to inspire discussion about growing from a toddler to a child by asking questions such as: *Which teddy looks the youngest? Who is the smallest in your family? Is the smallest person in your family also the youngest? Have you got any tops or trousers at home that are too small? Why are they too small, have they shrunk or have you grown bigger?*

Follow-up activities
● Provide the children with the CD-ROM and encourage them to complete the on-screen activity 'Dress the teddies'. The activity involves sorting and matching two sets of clothes to dress two different-sized bears.
● Read the poem 'Grown out of' on page 93.
● Help the children to construct eight 'life-sized' picture cards by drawing round four real T-shirts and four real pairs of shorts, in four different sizes (for example, toddler, child, teenager and adult) onto eight large sheets of card. Help the children to paint and decorate the clothing shapes to create a set of eight large playing cards for matching and sorting floor games.

Differentiation
Help younger or less able children with the practical challenge of cutting out the picture cards. Invite older or more able children to use two photocopiable pages to construct sixteen picture cards for playing games such as Pairs and Snap.

ON THE CD-ROM
● On-screen activity 'Dress the teddies'
● Photocopiable sheet 'Growing bigger'
● Poem 'Grown out of'

Growing bigger

● Cut into eight sections.

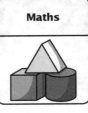

themes for early years

Body building

What you need
One body outline from the photocopiable sheet 'Building a body' on page 17 for each child; pencils; dice numbered 1 to 6; shaker.

What to do
Give each child a copy of the body outline and a pencil. Ask them to point to each number on their sheet as you call it out. Then go through the body parts (on the sheet) and ask them to point to these. Explain to them that they are going to take turns to throw the dice and that when they do so they should call out the number they have thrown, and then draw over the dotted lines of the body shape which matches the number on the dice. They should only draw round one shape at a time; therefore they must throw numbers 3, 4 and 5 twice. If they throw a number that has already been used up they either have to wait until their next turn or they can continue throwing the dice until they get a number they haven't yet thrown. The rules depend on the age and patience of the children. When they have outlined the whole body they can fill in the features of the face.

Discussion
Ask the children whether they would have been able to play this game when they were babies. Why not? Talk about the skills that they have used in playing this game. They have recognised numbers, held a pencil and drawn with it, and used the dice and shaker. What other things have they learned since they became old enough to go to school/nursery/playgroup?

Follow-up activities
● Help the children make a jigsaw from the body outline.
● Tell the story of 'The Gingerbread Man' (Traditional) and then hold a cookery session to bake some gingerbread men.
● Read the story *Funnybones* by Janet and Allan Ahlberg (Mammoth).
● Sing the action song 'Growing up' on page 83.

Differentiation
Help younger or less able children by playing along side them. Encourage older or more able children to play a body-building game that involves drawing each part themselves, without the pre-drawn outline. Players need to throw a 1 at first to draw the main body before moving on to the other parts.

STEPPING STONE
Use some number names accurately in play.

EARLY LEARNING GOAL
Recognise numerals 1 to 9. (MD)

ASSESSMENT
Do the children listen to instructions, take turns and play fairly?

ON THE CD-ROM
● Photocopiable page 'Building a body'
● Song 'Growing up'

Building a body

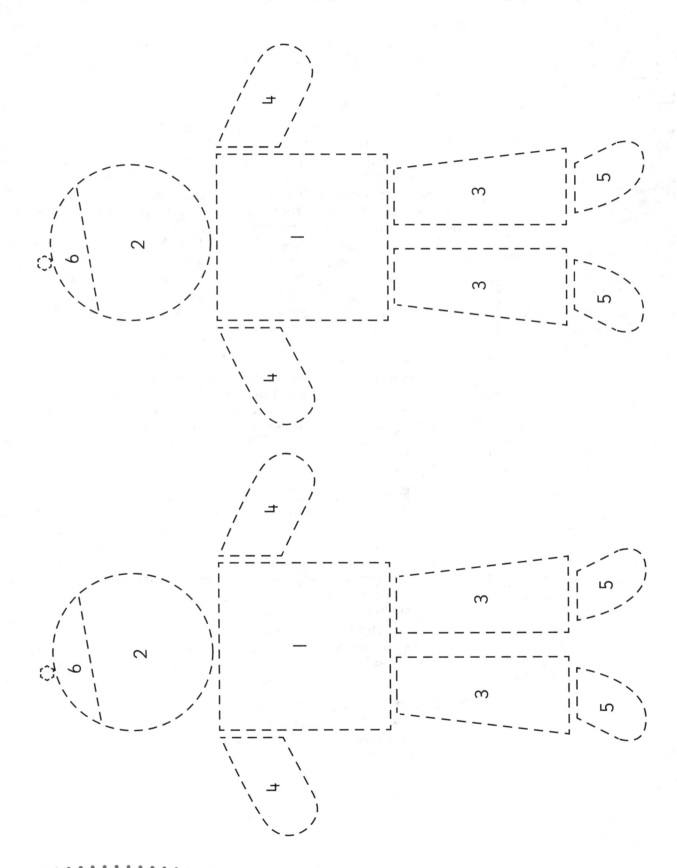

Art and craft

STEPPING STONE
Show care and concern for others, for living things and the environment.

EARLY LEARNING GOAL
Consider the consequences of their words and actions for themselves and others. (PSED)

ASSESSMENT
Do the children show signs of considering the consequences of their words and actions?

For my friend

What you need
A square of white paper (approximately 20cm × 20cm); pencils; felt-tipped pens; pastel and wax crayons.

What to do
Help the children to each do the following:
Fold the paper square in half diagonally and then in half again. Open it out so that you can see the middle of the square where the folds meet. Fold each corner into this middle point and press down the edges (see illustration 1). Now fold the new corners into the middle of this smaller square (see illustration 2), pressing the edges hard each time. Decorate the four triangles, holding them down to stop them from springing up. Try to make each triangle look the same with a line or circle going through all the triangles (illustration 3). Open out these triangles and decorate the layer underneath in similar fashion. Open out this second layer of triangles and write 'from …' (child's name) in the middle of the square. Finally, fold all the triangles up again, turn the present over and write the name of the friend receiving the present on the outside. Give the folded surprise to your friend.

Discussion
Try to help the children to understand that giving does not always concern material things. The most valuable thing that we can give to each other is our time, like the time that they have just spent in making a surprise for their friend. If their friend was pleased with the gift, how did he or she show it? Discuss the importance of friendship.

1.

2.

3.

Follow-up activities
● Let the children play a game of Tag outside with friends.
● Tell the children to play Follow-my-leader behind you – going slowly, quickly, hopping, skipping and jumping.
● Ask the children to take ten construction blocks and share them out between them. How many will they each have?
● Two friends can play on a see-saw and sing 'See-saw Marjorie Daw' (Traditional).
● If the children could give someone a lovely present, what would it be and who would they give it to?

Differentiation
Help younger or less able children to manipulate the folds. Encourage older or more able children to cut out the original square of paper to their choice of size.

Role play

When I'm grown up

What you need
An assortment of dressing-up clothes; hats and wigs; props (such as an umbrella, a walking stick, a handbag, jewellery, toy stethoscope); small suitcase; a full-length mirror (if possible).

What to do
Allow the children to go through the range of clothes and props. Ask them to choose the clothes that they might wear when they are grown up and have a job. Give the children a free rein when choosing their outfits, even if they look nothing like a person doing the job. When they have all chosen something to wear, call the group together to guess what everyone is dressed up as. Sing the following song to the tune of 'Lavender's Blue', and allow individual children to sing the part of their 'character'.

When I grow up dilly dilly,
I'm going to be,
A doctor in white (a plumber who mends,
a pop star who sings, and so on) dilly dilly.
You wait and see.

Let the children keep their dressing-up clothes on for the rest of the session while they carry out their normal routine. Encourage them to put the clothes away carefully at the end.

Discussion
Talk about what the children's parents and grandparents do either at home or out at work. Do the children know what people actually do when they work in an office, a hospital, an orchestra or other positions? Why do people work? Discuss jobs that require special clothes or uniforms and why these might be needed.

Follow-up activities
● Play a game of job association – hold up different equipment such as a spanner, a hair roller, a rolling pin, a garden trowel, a calculator and a thermometer, and ask: *Who uses this?*
● Help the children to act out a little story in their dressing-up clothes.
● Provide the children with the CD-ROM and discuss the photograph showing adults in uniforms and work clothes.

Differentiation
Help younger or less able children with practical challenges such as fastening buttons and doing up zips. Encourage older or more able children to perform short plays and scenarios in front of parents, carers, friends and peers.

ON THE CD-ROM
● Photograph showing adults in uniforms/work clothes.

Art and craft

themes for early years

Making handprints

What you need
A copy of the photocopiable sheet 'Big hands, little hands' on page 21; paint; shallow trays; pens; pencils.

Preparation
Organise an area in your setting for making handprints. Arrange for the children to invite a parent, carer, adult friend or adult relative into your setting, at an agreed time. Encourage the children to help their visitor make a handprint onto a copy of the photocopiable page 'Big hands, little hands'. Leave the prints to dry thoroughly.

What to do
When the adult handprints are dry, invite the children to make their own little handprint on top of the big handprint using a contrasting colour. Leave to dry thoroughly. Join in saying the rhyme on the photocopiable page: *One big handprint and a tiny one too. This is me and that is you.* Help the children to label the big hand with the name of the person whose hand was used to make the print and the little handprint with their own name. Invite the children to give the handprint to the named adult as a very special keepsake.

Discussion
Talk about how we change as we grow from a child to an adult, for example, we get taller, our hands get bigger, our feet get bigger, we weigh more. Can the children identify other obvious changes?

Follow-up activities
- Invite the children to make a second keepsake, but this time their own handprint will be the 'big hand'. Encourage them to invite younger siblings, friends or relatives into your setting, at a pre-arranged time, to create the 'little handprints'. Help the children to label the big handprint with their own name and the little hand with the name of the younger child whose hand was used to make the print.
- Make some colourful footprints using bare feet or the soles of old, clean shoes. Compare the sizes of the prints and use them to create an interesting display around your setting.

Differentiation
Help younger or less able children to copy or trace the names onto the keepsake. Encourage older or more able children to write the names with a high degree of independence.

ON THE CD-ROM
- Photocopiable sheet 'Big hands, little hands'

Big hands, little hands

● Print a child's hand on top of a larger handprint.

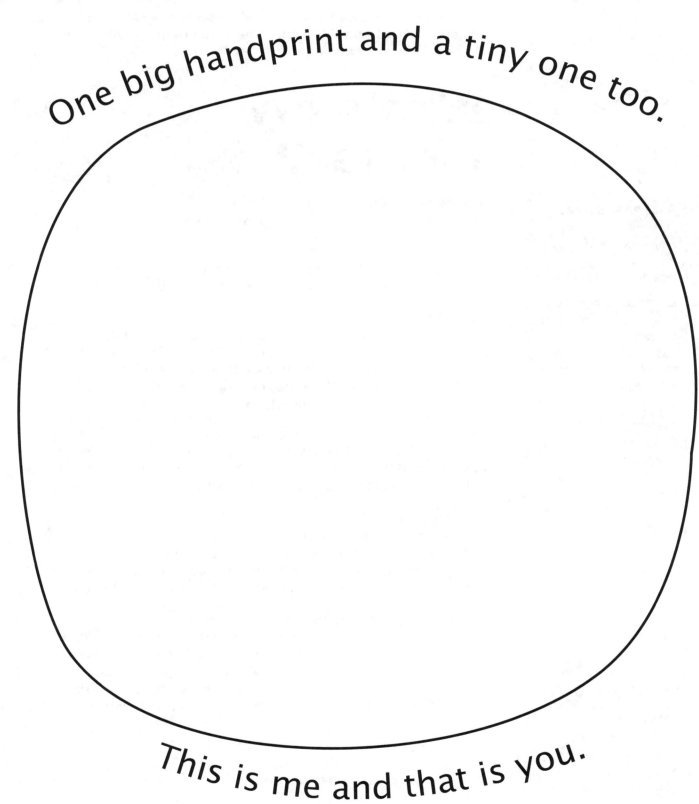

One big handprint and a tiny one too.

This is me and that is you.

Growth in animals

This chapter on animal growth will enable the children to look for similarities and differences between their growing up and that of different animals.

Sound

Who's my mother?

What you need
The photocopiable sheet 'Whose baby is it?' on page 23; scissors.

Preparation
Copy the photocopiable sheet onto card and cut out the pictures to make a set of eight animal cards. Work with a group of five children.

What to do
Divide the cards into parents and offspring. Give four of the children a parent card each and tell them not to show it to the others. The fifth child chooses one of the offspring cards and keeps it hidden too. This child now goes to one of the 'parents' who makes the sound of the animal on their card. If it matches his offspring card he will repeat the noise to show he has found his parent. If the parent sound doesn't match his animal he should move on to the next 'parent' until he finds the sound that does. The newly-found parent exchanges his card for an offspring card, and the four other children change their parent cards. Each time an offspring finds a parent, the parent becomes the new offspring.

Discussion
The baby animals found their parents by making the same noises. Are there any other ways in which parents and offspring can recognise each other? Young animals often look just like their parents, but not always. Does a young chick look like a mother hen, or a tadpole like a frog?

Follow-up activities
- Encourage the children to take it in turns to use the CD-ROM, on-screen jigsaw activity 'Match the baby animals' to connect two separate pictures showing a baby animal and its parent.
- Distribute the photocopiable sheet 'Whose baby is it?'. Ask the children to draw lines to match the animal parent with its young.

Differentiation
Help younger or less able children to mimic the animal sounds during the game. Encourage older or more able children to make extra picture cards showing animals and their young for the game.

themes for early years

STEPPING STONE
Initiate a conversation, negotiate positions, pay attention to and take account of other's views.

EARLY LEARNING GOAL
Sustain attentive listening, responding to what they have heard by relevant comments, questions or actions. (CLL)

ASSESSMENT
Do the children listen attentively during the game and respond to what they hear by relevant comments, questions or actions?

ON THE CD-ROM
- On-screen activity 'Match the baby animals'
- Photocopiable sheet 'Whose baby is it?'

Whose baby is it?

● Match the adult animal to the baby animal.

Construction and malleable materials

themes for early years

Find the caterpillar

What you need

Pictures of caterpillars; paper in shades of green; real twigs and branches; large egg-carton trays; scissors; masking tape; pipe-cleaners; PVA glue; buttons or pieces of felt for eyes; different-coloured paints, brushes.

What to do

Let the children choose a place in the room where their 'caterpillar' is going to feed. Decorate this area with paper leaves and a selection of real twigs and branches. An adult should cut the egg cartons into sections. Help the children to join several egg carton sections together using masking tape to make a long, flexible, caterpillar shape. Choose the colour needed to paint the caterpillar so that it will blend in with the background of its 'feeding' place.

When the paint is dry, an adult should carefully make holes on either side of the head section. Help the children to thread the pipe-cleaner into one of the holes and out of the other to make the feelers. Stick on two buttons or bits of felt to serve as eyes. Place the caterpillar in its selected spot where it will be camouflaged.

Discussion

Have any of the children ever seen a real caterpillar? Caterpillars hatch from eggs laid by a butterfly or moth. What do they use to move? Although they have legs they do not use them for walking, but for clasping on to food and stalks. Caterpillars crawl along using their many muscles. Why are caterpillars difficult to find? (Camouflage.) For food they eat the leaves or fruit on which they have hatched. As they increase in size they shed their skins several times. Eventually, when they have eaten enough and are fully-grown, they spin a cocoon round themselves and rest while their body is changing.

Follow-up activities
- Compare the different lengths of the egg-carton caterpillars. How many segments do they each have?
- Ask the children to crawl along the floor like a caterpillar, squashing themselves up then stretching out again.
- Make a temporary home for caterpillars in a jar, with holes pierced in the lid. Add some twigs. After a couple of days of observation, release the caterpillars where they were found.
- Read *The Very Hungry Caterpillar* by Eric Carle (Puffin).
- Sing the song 'Caterpillar' on page 85.

Differentiation

Help younger or less able children to select paint colours to create a camouflaged effect with the background. Encourage older or more able children to paint an interesting pattern on their caterpillar model.

ON THE CD-ROM
- Song 'Caterpillar'

themes for early years

Butterfly blobs

What you need
Pictures and photographs of colourful butterflies; large pieces of plain paper; pencils; scissors; paint in primary colours (red, yellow and blue); brushes; palettes.

Preparation
Fold the paper in half and draw the outline of a butterfly wing up to the fold. Cut round the folded outline and unfold the paper to show two wings. Provide one butterfly shape for each child.

What to do
Observe a selection of pictures and photographs showing beautiful butterflies, including the photograph on the CD-ROM. Give the children a paper butterfly shape and ask them to fold one wing back under the other (back to how it was when you cut it out). Encourage them to explore mixing the red, yellow and blue paints to create shades of orange, green, purple and brown. Invite the children to paint 'blobs' of colour onto the one wing to make a pattern. Make sure they don't brush it across the paper. Now they can carefully bring out the other wing from underneath and fold it on top of the blobs they have made. Show them how to smooth gently over the top wing with their hands. Unfold the butterfly to show the symmetrical pattern on both wings. Leave the butterfly open to dry. Create a display by attaching individual butterfly shapes around your setting on the walls, ceiling, windows and doors.

Discussion
While a caterpillar is inside its cocoon it is changing into a pupa. Who can guess what crawls out of the cocoon when the pupa has fully grown? At first the butterfly is damp and soft and hangs from a stem to dry out and wait for its wings to stiffen. Do the children know what a butterfly is looking for when it flies away? It lands on a brightly coloured flower and can detect whether there is any nectar (a sweet sugary liquid) inside the flower. Butterflies often fly to flowers that are the same colour as they are. Can the children think why this is?

STEPPING STONE
Explore what happens when they mix colours.

EARLY LEARNING GOAL
Explore colour, texture, shape, form and space in two or three dimensions. (CD)

ASSESSMENT
Were the children willing and able to explore what happens when they mix colours?

Follow-up activities
- Tuck one of your butterfly wings underneath the other and hold the straight edge of the patterned wing up against a mirror. What can you see?
- Decorate the underneath of your butterfly wings with green blobs to make them blend in with the leaves.
- Flap your arms like butterfly wings. Raise your 'wings' above your head like a butterfly does when it's asleep.
- Make some butterfly cakes (small sponge cakes with wings cut out and placed on top).

ON THE CD-ROM
- Photograph of a butterfly

Differentiation
Help younger or less able children to mix the colours. Encourage older or more able children to fold and cut the paper butterfly shapes.

themes for early years

Life cycle of a frog

What you need
CD-ROM photograph showing a frog; internet access to find pictures of
frogspawn and tadpoles; the photocopiable sheet 'Tadpoles to frogs' on
page 27; scissors; paper fastener; colouring pens; pencils.

Preparation
Copy the photocopiable sheet on to card to provide one for each child.

What to do
Encourage the children to colour in the pictures on the photocopiable
sheet 'Tadpoles to frogs'. They should use the CD-ROM photograph of
a frog and the internet pictures of frogspawn and tadpoles as a visual
reference. Talk about the illustrations on the photocopiable page and
help the children to identify the pictures. Invite them to cut out the
disc and pointer from the sheet and help them to attach the pointer to
the centre of the disc using a paper fastener. Encourage the children
to move the pointer round the disc to show the correct order of events
that occur during the life cycle of a frog.

Discussion
Encourage the children to use the illustrations on the life-cycle disc and
the photographs to inspire discussion. Explain that when frogs have
laid their spawn they leave it floating in pond water until it hatches.
Observe the pictures of the tadpoles and explain that the tadpole's
tail starts to shrink as soon as its legs begin to grow. Encourage the
children to describe the similarities and differences between a tadpole
and a frog and ask questions such as: *Which tadpoles most resemble
frogs? Which tadpoles least resemble frogs? What features does a frog
have that a tadpole does not have?*

Follow-up activities
● Say the rhyme 'The tadpole' on page 90.
● Sing the song 'Tadpole' on page 86.
● Set up a pond life display (see page 76).
● Help the children to create a 3D scene for the models using craft
  materials such as shiny paper or blue Cellophane to represent a
  pond, real stones and pebbles for the edging, and green fabric
  or paper shapes for imaginary weeds and plants.
● Say this tongue twister with the children: *Two teeny tiny tadpoles
  turn and twist their tails.*

Differentiation
Help younger or less able children to name and identify the pictures
on the life-cycle disc and photographs. Encourage older or more able
children to describe the life cycle of a frog in their own words.

Tadpoles to frogs

● Spin the counter arm. Look at the picture and answer the question.

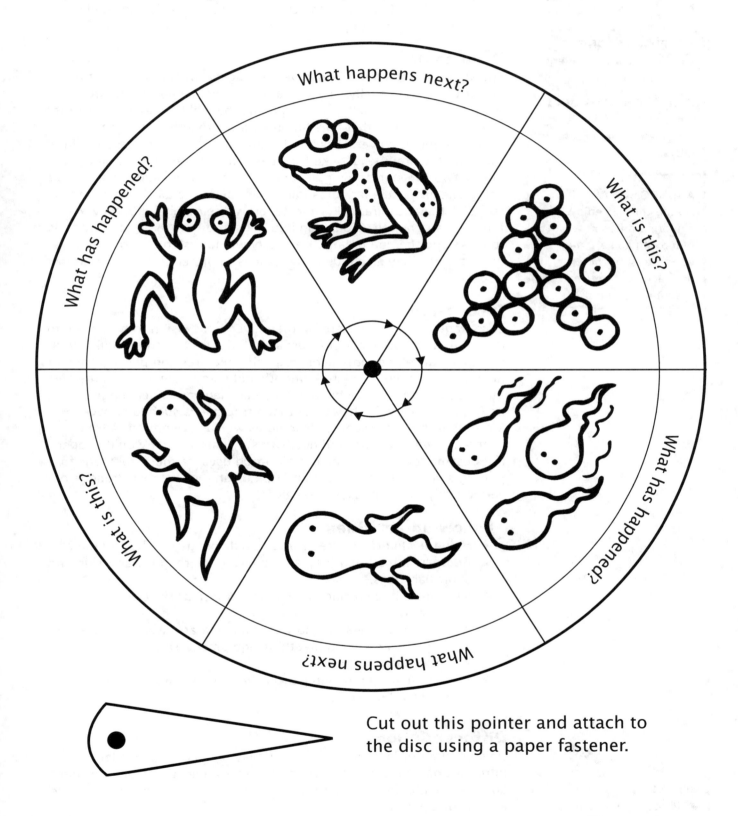

Cut out this pointer and attach to the disc using a paper fastener.

themes for early years

Leap frog

STEPPING STONE
Experiment with different ways of moving.

EARLY LEARNING GOAL
Move with confidence, imagination and in safety. (PD)

ASSESSMENT
Do the children enjoy exploring different ways of moving and are they willing to show others their achievements or describe their ideas?

What you need
An area outside that allows the children to move freely and safely; frogspawn; bowl of tadpoles or pictures.

What to do
Encourage the children to observe the frogspawn and talk about the way it wobbles like jelly. In a safe area outside, invite the children to gather together in small groups to mime the wobbly movements of the frogspawn. Suggest that they link their arms together and show them how to tremble, quiver, shake and shudder. They can drift around in their wobbly groups, just like frogspawn floating around a pond. Soon one or two can start to wriggle away from the group and swim around using one arm like a tadpole's tail. When they have all changed into tadpoles they can gradually start to 'grow' their limbs until they have four legs and no tail. Crouching like frogs, they can leap from lily pads to rocks and then on to land. Here they will find slugs, worms and insects. They may also hide under stones to protect themselves from larger animals.

Discussion
Encourage the children to recall the movement session to help them to describe the movements of frogspawn, tadpoles and frogs. Talk about the appearance of a tadpole or frog using pictures and photographs to help. For example, the skin is smooth and shiny, its eyes are large and bulge out, its feet are webbed and its back legs are much longer than its front legs. Why do they think that a frog needs such long back legs? Stress that they use them for leaping as well as swimming. A frog is a land and water animal and needs to stay damp. What would happen if it became too dry? (It would die.) A frog uses its short front legs for putting slugs or worms into its mouth. It can flick its sticky tongue out very quickly to catch insects to eat.

Follow-up activities
● Help the children to create a textured collage of a frog or toad.
● Compare a toad to a frog: a toad has a dry, rough, warty skin and short back legs.
● Sing 'Five Little Freckled Frogs' from *Knock at the Door* by Jan Betts (Ward Lock).
● A frogman is a person who works under water wearing a wet suit and flippers and using breathing equipment. Draw a frogman in an underwater scene.
● Say the rhyme 'Frogs jump' from *Up, Up and Away* by Derek Pearson (OUP).

Differentiation
Help younger or less able children by playing Follow-my-leader to introduce new movements, actions or mimes. Encourage older or more able children to devise short sequences of movements or to mirror the actions of a partner.

ON THE CD-ROM
● Photograph of a frog

themes for early years

Incy Wincy

STEPPING STONE
Express needs and feelings in appropriate ways.

EARLY LEARNING GOAL
Respond to significant experiences, showing a range of feelings when appropriate. (PSED)

ASSESSMENT
Are the children happy to join in the discussions and are they comfortable in expressing their thoughts, views, needs and feelings?

What you need
Pictures of spiders and webs; pair of scissors; a piece of card, blunt-ended needles and thick black thread for each child.

Preparation
An adult should punch holes, at set intervals, along a web of lines, pre-drawn onto a square of card for each child.

What to do
Sing together the nursery rhyme 'Incy Wincy spider' (both verses). Look at the pictures of spiders and webs and point out how the spoke pattern looks like a bicycle wheel. Give each child their own card and threaded needle and show them how to make stitches in and out of the holes. It doesn't matter if the web gets to be a bit lop-sided or tangled, after all, young spiders that are learning how to spin may not have perfect webs!

When the children have finished sewing (they may want to use more than one thread), knot the ends and store the needles away carefully.

Discussion
Have the children ever struggled to do something, like the spider that was washed down the spout? Did they feel like giving up? Consider sayings such as, *Try, try, and try again* and *Practice makes perfect*. Talk about what these sayings mean. Encourage the children to consider how they can help others who are younger or new to your setting.

Follow-up activity
- Draw a thick black spider on the sewn web card.
- Count how many legs a spider has. How many legs do two spiders have?
- Can the children scuttle across the floor very quickly just like a spider?
- Watch the film clip of a spider weaving a web on the CD-ROM.
- Try to spot a spider's web sparkling with morning dew drops.
- Say the action rhyme 'I Have a Little Spider' from *This Little Puffin* compiled by Elizabeth Matterson (Penguin).
- Sing 'Under a Web' from *Count Me In* (A&C Black).

Differentiation
Provide younger or less able children with hand-over-hand support during the sewing stage. Encourage older or more able children to draw the web of lines onto the squares of card.

ON THE CD-ROM
- Film clip showing a spider making a web.

Natural discovery

themes for early years

Cracking good eggs

What you need

A copy of the photocopiable sheet 'The cracking egg' on page 31; internet access to find pictures of chicks hatching; pens; pencils; scissors; strip of card; tape.

What to do

Provide the children with the internet pictures showing an egg cracking and a chick hatching. Talk about the images and encourage the children to describe them.

Provide the children with a copy of the photocopiable sheet 'The cracking egg' and help them to cut out the pictures and to secure them, in the correct order, along a strip card. Help the children to bend and tape the strip of card to create a simple 'roundabout' booklet. Encourage the children to turn the booklet round and around to reveal the repeated sequence of events that occurs during the chicken and egg life cycle.

Discussion

Encourage the children to use their roundabout booklets to help them describe the sequence of events that occur during the chicken and egg life cycle. Ask questions such as *What happens when the chick has fully grown inside the shell? How does the chick get out of the shell? What does a baby chick grow into?* and *Where do eggs come from?*

Follow-up activities
● Sing the nursery rhyme 'Humpty Dumpty'.
● Invite the children to decorate hard-boiled eggs using coloured pens and collage materials.
● Look at an empty bird's nest then try to make one from some straw and mud.
● Compare the size and weight of a duck and a goose egg to that of a hen's egg.
● Say the poem 'Eggs for breakfast' from *The Book of a Thousand Poems* (Collins).
● Crack some egg whites into a bowl and invite the children to help make some meringues.

Differentiation

Help younger or less able children to place the photocopiable pictures in the correct order along the strip of card. Encourage older or more able children to draw some of their own pictures for the roundabout book using the internet pictures as a visual resource.

The cracking egg

● Cut out the pictures. Put them into the correct order.

themes for early years

Caterpillar to butterfly

STEPPING STONE
Draw and paint, sometimes giving meaning to marks.

EARLY LEARNING GOAL
Write their own names and other things such as labels and captions and begin to form simple sentences, sometimes using punctuation. (CLL)

ASSESSMENT
Can the children describe what they see in pictures, drawings and paintings? Are they willing to attempt to write simple labels, captions or sentences about pictures or things they have observed?

What you need
A card copy of the photocopiable sheet 'Butterfly jigsaw' on page 33; child scissors; pens; pencils; internet access for images of a caterpillar and chrysalis; CD-Rom photograph showing a butterfly.

Preparation
Copy the photocopiable sheet on to card, one for each child.

What to do
Give each child a card copy of the photocopiable sheet 'Butterfly jigsaw' and invite them to colour it in. Help them to cut around the lines to create a simple, circular jigsaw with four sections. Ask the children to identify the pictures in each section: caterpillar eggs, fully grown caterpillar; a chrysalis; a butterfly. Invite the children to mix up the four pieces, then reassemble the jigsaw to show, in the correct order, the four main events that take place when a caterpillar changes into a butterfly. They should use the arrows printed in each section of the jigsaw to help them to identify the correct sequence of events. Invite the children to glue the jigsaw onto backing paper and to label each section with a word or caption to describe the picture. Reinforce understanding by inviting them to draw or paint the sequence of events on a large circle of paper, pre-divided into four equal sections.

Discussion
Look at the jigsaw pictures and paintings with the children. Ask them to describe each picture. Can they recall the sequence of events? Ask questions for the children to consider, for example, *Does the caterpillar or butterfly lay the eggs? Does a caterpillar or butterfly hatch out of the eggs? Does a caterpillar or butterfly hatch out of the chrysalis?*

Follow-up activities
● Arrange a minibeast hunt in a safe and suitable area.
● Invite the children to take photographs of minibeasts in their own habitat, for example, on leaves, under logs, in the grass.
● Help the children to draw and write out the names of minibeasts seen around your setting.
● Make some pretend eggs, caterpillars, chrysalis and butterflies using Plasticine, or salt-dough.
● Draw an imaginary minibeast and make up a name for it.
● Sing the song 'Caterpillar' on page 85.

Differentiation
Colour and cut out an enlarged card copy of the photocopiable sheet 'Butterfly jigsaw' for younger children to use as a group. Encourage older or more able children to write simple sentences about the sequence of events shown in the jigsaw.

ON THE CD-ROM
● Photocopiable sheet 'Butterfly jigsaw'
● Photograph of a butterfly
● Song 'Caterpillar'

Butterfly jigsaw

● Cut out the sections. Put them together to show the life cycle of a butterfly.

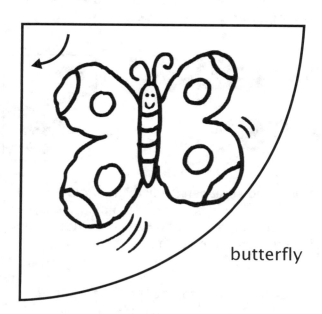

butterfly

caterpillar

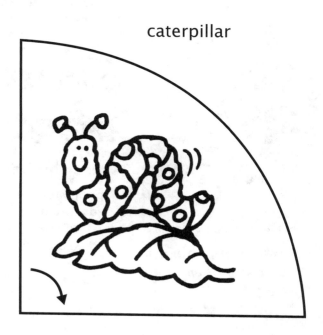

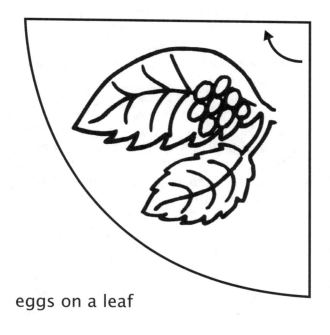

eggs on a leaf

chrysalis

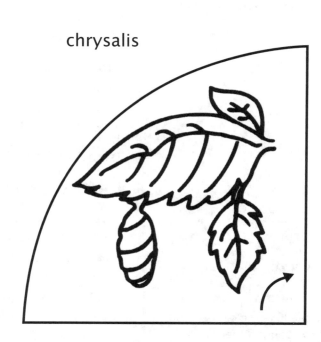

Seeds and plants

In this chapter children will sow seeds and watch plants growing from them. They will learn that plants need water, warmth and light just as much as they themselves do.

themes for early years

STEPPING STONE
Make constructions, collages, paintings, drawings and dances.

EARLY LEARNING GOAL
Explore colour, texture, shape, form and space in two or three dimensions. (CD)

ASSESSMENT
Were the children willing to explore and experiment by creating several different patterns and styles before gluing the seeds in place?

ON THE CD-ROM
● Photograph of a sunflower showing the seeds in the centre
● Song 'A seed'

From small beginnings

Art and craft

What you need

Paper plates; pencils; PVA glue and spreaders; collection of different seeds (dried peas, kidney beans, black-eyed beans, pumpkin seeds, mustard seeds, peppercorns, wheat grain, sunflower seeds, rice, bird seeds, apple pips, conkers and acorns and so on).

What to do

Let the children handle, and experiment with, the different types of seeds, arranging them in different patterns on their plates before deciding on their final arrangement. Observe them at all times to ensure that they do not try to eat the seeds.

Encourage the children to glue only a small area of the plate at a time. Start with a patch in the middle, add one type of seed, press them into the glue and shake off the surplus. Now glue another small section or a circular area around the central patch and add another type of seed. Repeat this until the plate is covered with seeds and leave it flat until the glue has dried. Use the decorated plates as mobiles, or display several plates together on the wall.

Discussion

Explain to the children that these seeds all come from flowering plants, and that they would grow into new plants given the right conditions. The wheat grain would grow into wheat and the dried bean into a bean plant. Compare the difference between an apple pip and the seed (stone) that comes from a peach or plum tree.

Follow-up activities
● Put the leftover seeds into tight-lidded pots to make shakers.
● Cut open two apples, extract the seeds and see if the apples have the same amount of pips.
● Sing the song 'A seed' on page 85.

Differentiation

Invite younger or less able children to create a random pattern. Encourage older or more able children to create a symmetrical pattern.

themes for early years

Seeds move home

What you need

A safe and secure area outside; dried poppy head on its stalk (or a pepper pot filled with dry sand); sycamore seeds (or a small strip of lightweight paper); a dandelion clock; dried pea or bean pods.

What to do

Show the children how the poppy would move in the wind, shaking its head and scattering seeds (alternatively shake fine sand from the pepper pot into the air). Invite the children to blow a dandelion clock and to watch as the seeds blow away in the wind. Encourage the children to drop sycamore seeds or paper strips from a height to observe them spin in the air.

For the movement session, the children can choose whether to shake, drift or spin in the way that seeds do in the wind. They can move like birds and squirrels do, eating, dropping and hiding nuts. Remind them how animals act when they hear a sudden noise and are frightened.

Pull open the bean or pea pods and let the children make the same bursting movements as seeds that fly out of pods.

Discussion

When seeds are ripe they leave their parent plant to grow into new plants. What would happen if all the seeds started to grow in the same place? Some seeds can travel a long way from the parent plant so that they don't have to compete for light and water. Can the children suggest ways in which the seeds travel? The wind helps move dandelion seeds that float like parachutes, sycamore seeds spin through the air like helicopters, a poppy head scatters its tiny seeds as the wind blows it backwards and forwards.

Follow-up activities
- The children can work in pairs and take it in turns to guess which type of seed dispersal their partner is miming.
- Sing and play 'Here We Go Gathering Nuts in May' (Traditional).
- Hang a pine cone outside and watch it open in dry weather to let its seeds drop.
- Sing the song 'Dandelion clock' on page 82.

Differentiation

Invite younger or less able children to join in the movement session in pairs. Encourage older or more able children to create short dance sequences using ideas gathered during the movement session.

ON THE CD-ROM
- Song 'Dandelion clock'

themes for early years

Roots and shoots

STEPPING STONE
Show an awareness of change

EARLY LEARNING GOAL
Look closely at similarities, differences, patterns and change. (KUW)

ASSESSMENT
Are the children interested in examining plants and finding out about how they grow?

What you need
A very tall glass jar; damp sand; tablespoon; paper towels; four dry broad beans; water; label; pencil; an adult's clean sock.

Preparation
Soak two of the dry broad beans in cold water for 24 hours before the activity.

What to do
Let the children compare the two dry and the two soaked beans. Ask them to help line the inside of the jar with two dry paper towels. Encourage them to spoon the sand down inside the paper (almost to the top) to hold it in place. Using the spoon handle, ease two spaces (on opposite sides) between the side of the jar and the paper. Help the children to position the two soaked beans in these spaces, one vertically and one horizontally with the tip uppermost as shown in the illustration. Invite the children to carefully pour a little water down the sides of the jar to wet the sand and paper lining.

Encourage the children to use the label to record the starting date before covering the jar with the sock.

Discussion
Examine the beans every day with the children and talk about any changes that take place. When the beans have sprouted (after about three days), remove the sock and continue observing the seeds. Make sure that the lining paper is always damp. After about one week, green leaves will start to show. Encourage the children to record the growth of the beans using a camera or by drawing pictures at regular intervals. Display the pictures on the wall or in an album to help the children recall what has happened.

Follow-up activities
● Plant the growing bean in the garden and let it climb up a cane.
● Provide the children with the CD-ROM and encourage them to complete the on-screen activity titled 'How a plant grows'. The activity involves sequencing a set of pictures that show a plant during various stages of growth.
● Watch the roots growing on the CD-ROM film clip.
● Help the children to set up a display (see page 77).

ON THE CD
● Film clip 'Roots growing'
● On-screen activity 'How a plant grows'

Differentiation
Provide younger or less able children with one-to-one support during each stage of the activity. Encourage older or more able children to use writing to record the changes that occur to the beans.

Food

themes for early years

STEPPING STONE
Talk about what is seen and what is happening.

EARLY LEARNING GOAL
Look closely at similarities, differences, patterns and change. (KUW)

ASSESSMENT
Are the children willing to share observations, views and feelings about what they have seen?

Growing needs

What you need
Cress seeds; four shallow bowls; two plates that will completely cover the top of the dishes; paper towels; cling film; water; labels; pencil.

What to do
Invite the children to place a thick layer of paper towels into the bottom of each bowl. Help them to dampen the towels and to sprinkle a teaspoonful of seeds into each. Cover two of the bowls with the plates and the other two with some cling film. Help the children place one plate-covered dish and one film-covered dish inside a fridge.
Place the other two dishes in a warm room in good light. Help the children to label each dish with the starting date and the place where it is kept. Look at the seeds every day for two weeks. When the children look at the seeds under the plates, encourage them to replace the plates quickly to stop light getting to them. Ensure that the paper towels are kept damp all the time. Help the children to keep a record of what is happening to the seeds, using pictures, photographs, and writing or by speaking into a tape-recorder.

Discussion
What do seeds need to grow into healthy plants? The seeds under the plate in the warm place will grow more than those under the cling film. Seeds like to sprout in the dark. Which seedlings look healthiest after a week? Once seeds have sprouted they need light to grow green leaves. If they are kept in the dark for too long they will grow yellow and straggly. What has happened to the two dishes of seeds in the fridge? Seeds will not start to grow if they are not warm enough.

Follow-up activities
- Draw a face on half an empty eggshell. Fill it with damp kitchen paper. Sprinkle on some mustard seeds. In a few days your shell face will have hair on top.
- Make sandwiches with the mustard and cress.
- Say the action poem 'A seedy story' on page 87.
- Plant some carrot seeds in deep pots outside.
- Watch the film clip on the CD-ROM showing a plant growing.

Differentiation
Help younger or less able children to grow one successful bowl of seeds. At various stages during the activity encourage older or more able children to anticipate what will happen next.

ON THE CD-ROM
- Film clip showing a hyacinth growing
- Poem 'A seedy story'

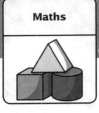

themes for early years

STEPPING STONE
Order two or three items by length.

EARLY LEARNING GOAL
Use language such as 'greater', 'smaller', 'heavier' or 'lighter' to compare quantities. (MD)

ASSESSMENT
Do the children use language such as 'longer', 'shorter', 'smallest' and 'tallest' to describe the paper stems?

Sizing stems

What you need
Vase containing flowers of different colours; paper towels; large piece of paper; narrow strips (about 3cm wide) of white paper at least the length of the tallest flower; scissors and a pencil for each child; wax crayons; glue and spreaders.

What to do
Help the children lay the flowers on top of the paper strips. Show them how to mark the length of each stem with a pencil, not including the flower head, (see illustration). Help the children to trim away the excess strips of paper. Encourage them to colour the remaining strip (which is the length of the stem). Replace the flowers in the vase.

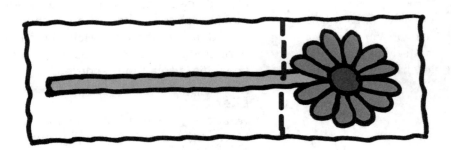

Let the children arrange the paper strip 'stems' in size order, starting with either the shortest or longest. Glue these ordered strips on to the large piece of paper. Invite the children to draw or paint pretty flower heads to place on top of the paper stems to create a colourful display. Label the display with words such as 'The size of our flower stems'.

Discussion
Explain that a stem is part of the shoot that grows upwards from a seed. As well as holding flower heads for insects to visit, a stem also supports the leaves of a plant. Food and water are sucked up the stem like juice being sucked up through a drinking straw.

Follow-up activities
● Cut the top 3cm from a stick of celery and keep this piece wrapped and moist. Make a clean cut at the base of the remaining stick and stand it in 6cm of red coloured water (use food dye). After four hours, cut the stick in half and compare the inside to the wrapped piece.
● Sing 'The sunflower song' on page 84.
● Stand two children back to back. Who is the tallest and who is the shortest of the pair?

ON THE CD-ROM
● Song 'The sunflower song'

Differentiation
Help younger or less able children to compare the length of two stems. Help older or more able children to measure the paper stems using a ruler.

Art and craft

themes for early years

Leaves have veins

STEPPING STONE
Work creatively on a large or small scale.

EARLY LEARNING GOAL
Explore colour, texture, shape, form and space in two or three dimensions. (CD)

ASSESSMENT
Are the children keen to explore differences in colour, shape, texture and pattern?

What you need
A collection of at least six different types of leaves (such as laurel, ivy, beech, cabbage, fern, conifer); six different coloured paints ready-mixed in pots with a brush in each; large sheet of painting paper for each child; pile of newspaper pages cut in half; wastepaper bin; damp cloth.

What to do
Let each child choose a leaf and a paint colour. Invite them to place their leaf with the vein side facing upwards on to a piece of newspaper, and then paint the surface of the leaf using the brush. Help them to place this leaf, with the painted side down, on to the painting paper. Put another piece of newspaper on top of the leaf and encourage the children to carefully rub their hand over it so that the leaf imprint will be left on the painting paper. Repeat the process with the different leaves, making prints on to the same piece of paper. Mount the leaf prints and display on the wall with a title such as 'Our leaf prints' or 'Leaves have veins'.

Discussion
Encourage the children to examine a wide range of different leaves. Talk about the different shapes, colours, sizes and textures of the leaves. Explain that all leaves have veins. The veins carry water around the plant. Some leaves are shiny, others are very pointed, but all are made in such a way that rain runs off them.

Follow-up activities
● Provide the children with the CD-ROM and encourage them to view the photograph showing leaves with clearly visible veins.
● Use different shades of green paint to give leaf prints a 'natural' look.
● Sort leaves into sets according to type, size, shape, dark or light colour.
● Compare the edges of leaves. Staple a leaf to a piece of paper and draw round its edge with a pencil.
● Can the children find the veins on their hands?

Differentiation
Invite younger or less able children to print the leaves randomly on the paper. Encourage older or more able children to arrange some leaf prints to form a pattern sequence.

ON THE CD-ROM
● Photograph of leaves with clearly visible veins

Thirsty roots

What you need
Three onions of approximately the same size; two tall glasses or vases with narrow necks; plant pot; bulb fibre or compost; jug of water; labels; pencil.

What to do
Let the children handle the onion bulbs and point out the dried-up root fibres at the base.

Help the children to pour enough water into one of the tall glasses so that when a bulb is placed in the neck of the glass it is only just slightly above the surface. Put the second bulb into the neck of the other glass that contains no water. Encourage the children to make a small depression in the bulb fibre in the plant pot, dampen it and then sit the third bulb in it. Help the children to place date labels onto the containers.

The roots of the bulb in the glass of water should start to grow within two or three days. After about two weeks, when the children can see the roots growing strongly in the glass, gently lift the bulb that is growing in the plant pot and invite the children to examine its roots. Encourage the children to compare the roots of the three bulbs.

Discussion
Talk about the different rates of growth of the three bulbs. Ask the children why one didn't grow at all. Tree roots are very strong. They branch out, and can push through hard earth to find water and food (minerals in the soil). If there is something in their way, they will either grow round it or push through it. Have the children ever seen cracked or lifted paving stones around the base of a tree? Are there any other reasons why tree roots need to be very strong? (To anchor the tree and prevent it from being blown over.)

Follow-up activities
- Use the photocopiable sheet 'Growing roots' on page 41 and ask the children to draw roots growing towards water. They can use a thick crayon to do this.
- Dramatise the story of 'The Enormous Turnip' (Ladybird Books).
- Cut through a bulb (use daffodil, tulip or crocus bulbs) lengthwise and look at the arrangement of the layers.
- Encourage the children to watch the film clip of the roots growing on the CD-ROM.

Differentiation
Help younger or less able children to observe and compare the bulbs. Encourage older or more able children to make a written or pictorial record of progress for each bulb.

Growing roots

● Draw in the roots as they branch out to find water.
Remember to go around the stones.

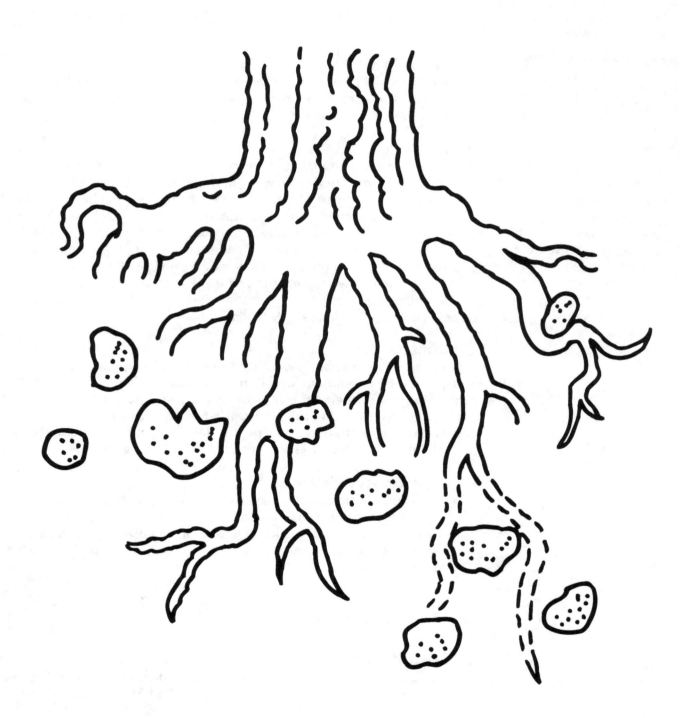

Natural discovery

STEPPING STONE
Show an interest in the world in which they live.

EARLY LEARNING GOAL
Find out about their environment, and talk about those features they like and dislike. (KUW)

ASSESSMENT
Do the children show an interest in the natural world by asking questions, making comments and responding to activities with enthusiasm?

New plants from old

What you need
Sprouting potatoes; sharp knife (adult use only); all-purpose compost; plant pots; tray; water.

Preparation
Five or six weeks in advance of this activity put some 'old' potatoes (with tough thick skins) in a cool, light (not sunny) room until they sprout white shoots of about 1cm in length.

What to do
Explain to the children that some plants can make new plants without the need for seeds. They can grow a new plant from a piece of themselves, such as part of a stem or a root. Potatoes can be grown in this way. Show the children the spouting potatoes. An adult should then cut the potatoes into three pieces, each containing at least one 'spout', 'shoot' or 'eye'. Help the children to half-fill each plant pot with compost and lay a potato piece on top of each. Cover with more compost and press down gently. Water the pots and leave them on a tray on a window-sill. Keep the compost moist at all times. The shoots should appear within a week and the leaves four days after that.

Discussion
Talk to the children about how other plants grow, for example, strawberry plants send out long thin stems across the ground called runners, new strawberry plants grow on the end of each runner. Buttercups also spread in this way. Daffodil bulbs grow baby bulbs around themselves to make new plants. Raspberry plants send out very long shoots underground, these 'suckers' grow into new plants.

Follow-up activities
● Plant three African violet leaves (with stalks attached) into a pot of damp compost. Place the pot in a secured transparent plastic bag. Leave it in a warm, light place until new plantlets start to grow after about five weeks. Remove the bag once they are growing well.
● Draw a picture of a garden covered in buttercups.
● Sing the song 'One potato, two potato' from *This Little Puffin* compiled by Elizabeth Matterson (Puffin).

Differentiation
Provide younger or less able children with one-to-one support during the planting stage. Encourage older or more able children to examine the potato 'shoots' with a magnifying glass.

Trees and flowers

The seasons of the year affect all living things. This chapter will help the children to watch these changes, and gain an understanding of the importance of trees and flowers.

themes for early years

Count the rings

Maths

What you need
Some pictures of different types and sizes of trees; some logs (with rough and smooth bark) of different diameters, split lengthwise; thin plain paper; drawing pins; short stubby wax crayons; soft pencils.

What to do
Count the rings or the lines on the different-shaped logs. Explain that the circles or lines of wood inside the logs show how many years old the tree was. Fix a piece of paper to each log with drawing pins. The children can use a soft pencil or the edge of a wax crayon to rub gently backwards and forwards until the lines of the wood show through, on to the paper. Each child can make a rubbing of a log cut crosswise and lengthwise. Help the children to try and discover how old one of the logs is by counting the rings.

Encourage the children to take it in turns to try the on-screen activity 'Tree pieces'. The activity involves counting rings on a set of tree stumps and placing them in order of age.

Discussion
What is the thickest part of the tree called? The trunk grows a little bit fatter and taller each year as the tree grows. Why are trees so important? They help to give us clean air to breathe and stop the soil from being washed away by the rain. Trees give us shelter from hot sun and from strong wind. Some trees have been growing for much longer than we have.

Follow-up activities
● Collect some fallen branches and twigs and lay them out in order of thickness.
● Make a collection of things found in the room that are made from wood.

Differentiation
Help younger or less able children to complete the activity on the CD-ROM. Encourage older or more able children to measure round some growing tree trunks with a piece of tape to compare their size.

themes for early years

The four seasons

What you need
The photocopiable sheet 'Wheelbarrow' on page 45 for each child; crayons or felt-tipped pens; variety of evergreen leaves; bag full of autumn leaves; glue and spreaders; safe area outside to collect leaves; wheelbarrow or garden sack.

What to do
Encourage the children to take it in turns to view the collage style photograph of a tree in four seasons on the CD-ROM. Talk about the image and ask the children to name and identify the four different seasons by observing the leaves within each section of the picture.

Take the children into the garden to collect some fallen autumn leaves to put into a wheelbarrow or garden sack. Show them places where they may pick some evergreen leaves safely. Once inside, let them examine both types of leaves and encourage them to feel them, listen to them and smell them. Give each child a copy of the photocopiable sheet 'Wheelbarrow' to colour, and then spread some glue in the area above it. Let them choose and stick some of the fallen leaves on to the paper to make a picture of a barrow brimming with autumn leaves.

Discussion
Ask the children to describe the look and feel of both types of leaves, such as thick or thin, rough or smooth, shiny or prickly, tough or delicate, waxy or dull. Listen to both types of leaves as they handle them – is it only the dry leaves that rustle? Let them compare the smell of the autumn leaves to the smell of the green leaves.

Follow-up activities
● Drag your feet through autumn leaves and listen to the sound they make.
● In spring, put a horse chestnut twig in a vase of water and watch the 'sticky buds' open out.
● Pack some autumn leaves into a bin bag. Leave the bag sealed for a few months then open it up to see how the leaves have broken down into compost.
● Fill a vase with a collection of evergreen leaves. Paint a picture of the different shapes and shades of green.

Differentiation
Invite younger or less able children to work in pairs to decorate the wheelbarrow outline. Encourage older or more able children to draw their own wheelbarrow outline.

Wheelbarrow

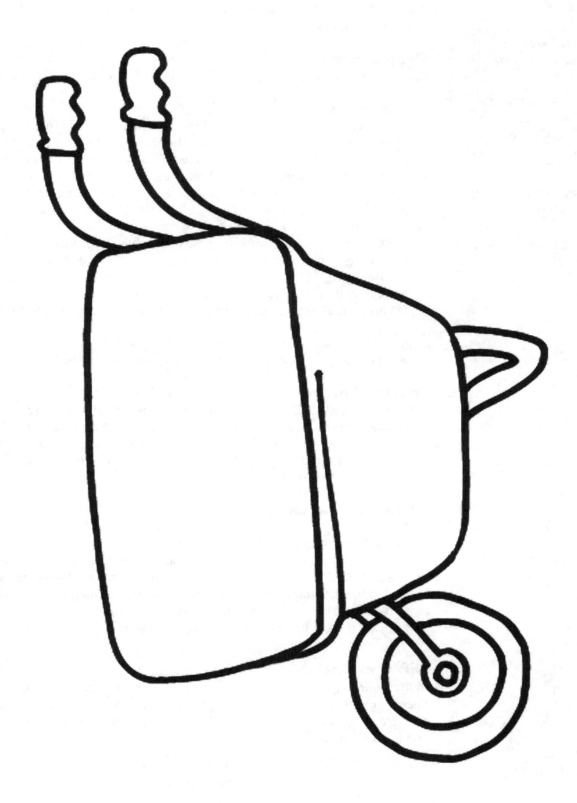

Sound

themes for early years

Tree life

What you need
The photocopiable sheet 'Our tree home' on page 47 for each child; crayons; scissors.

Preparation
Cut out the five separate picture cards on the photocopiable sheets.

What to do
Give a copy of the tree outline and the five picture cards to each child. Read through the creature names on the tree outline with the children. Tell them that you will give them 'clues' to help them to guess which creature, or thing, lives on or under a tree. When they think they know the answer to your clue they should pick a card and match it to the same word on the tree. After they have matched all the cards they can remove them and colour in the tree.

Possible clues to use with the photocopiable sheet include:
- A long thin creature with no legs that wriggles through the soil. (A worm.)
- A bird that likes to fly at night. (An owl.)
- An animal with a long furry tail that jumps from branch to branch. (A squirrel.)
- A place where birds lay their eggs. (A nest.)
- A creature that is very good at spinning. (A spider.)

Discussion
Trees provide shelter and food for many different animals and birds. Have the children heard of the dawn chorus? What does it sound like? What is their favourite animal sound? Can they imitate this sound? Encourage the children to select some percussion instruments to imitate different animal sounds?

Follow-up activities
- How many different types of birds can the children spot resting on the trees outside?
- Make a wormery in a large glass jar by layering soil, leaves and sand. Add some worms, then keep the jar covered – except when you have a quick look. You can tell if the worms have moved because the soil, sand and leaves will be all mixed up.
- Draw the outline shapes of different trees.

Differentiation
Invite younger children to play the game with an older partner. Encourage older or more able children to think of other tree creatures and draw them onto the tree outline, for example, woodlice, slugs, snails and mice.

ON THE CD-ROM
- Photocopiable sheet 'Our tree home'

Our tree home

● Match the pictures to the names.

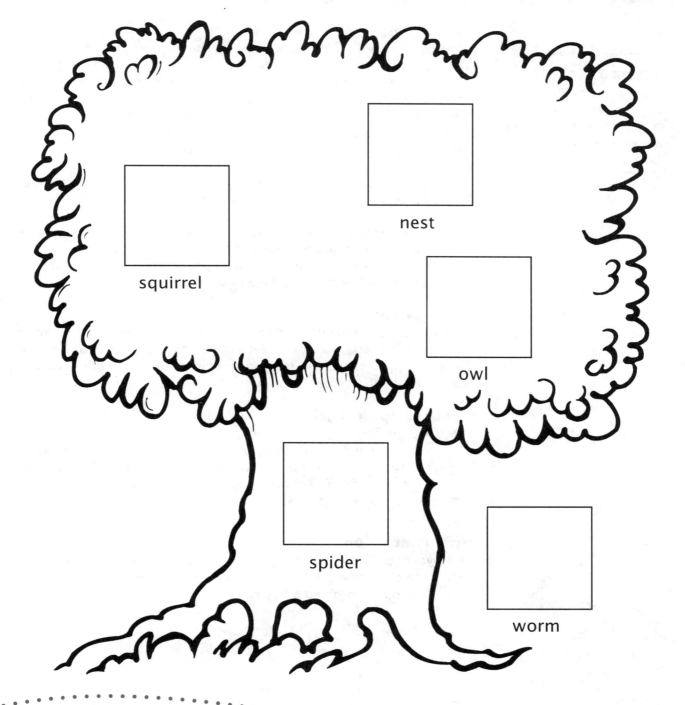

nest

squirrel

owl

spider

worm

Art and craft

Pretty petals

themes for early years

STEPPING STONE
Choose particular colours to use for a purpose.

EARLY LEARNING GOAL
Explore colour, texture, shape, form and space in two or three dimensions. (CD)

ASSESSMENT
Did the children think purposefully about the colours they were selecting and the shapes they were making?

What you need
Three different types of flowers with large single heads (one bell-shaped, one with a flat head and one rose); sheets of paper of different colours and textures; piece of card (approximate size A4) for each child; scissors and a pencil for each child; three pots of glue; six spreaders; felt-tipped pens.

Preparation
Fold all the pieces of card in half.

What to do
Show the children the three real flowers and encourage them to design their own flower using craft materials. Ask them to choose a sheet of paper in a particular texture and colour, and show them how to fold it into quarters. To make the petals, they can draw two petal shapes on the top piece of the folded paper. Holding all the layers of paper together they then cut round these shapes. They can cut out more petals in another colour to make a flower using two colours, or to make more flowers.

When they have decided how many petals they want to use for their flower head, they should arrange and glue them on to their own piece of folded card.

Some children may like to share their petals with friends and create flowers with multi-coloured heads. If they have left a gap in the middle of their flower they can colour it in with a felt-tipped pen. The finished work can be used as a card to give to someone.

Discussion
Did the real flower petals overlap or fit into each other? Did the paper flower petals overlap or fit into each other? Were all the petals on each flower the same shape and size? Talk about whom the children would like to give their summer card to.

Follow-up activities
● Help the children to write 'from …' inside their cards.
● Invite the children to take it in turns to use the CD-ROM, on-screen activity titled 'Make a flower' to design an imaginary flower using a selection of different petal shapes and leaves.
● Press some real flowers.

Differentiation
Invite younger or less able children to cut random petal shapes. Encourage older or more able children to use shades of one colour to create a colour co-ordinated flower.

ON THE CD-ROM
● On-screen activity titled 'Make a flower'

Art and craft

themes for early years

STEPPING STONE
Begin to differentiate colours.

EARLY LEARNING GOAL
Explore colour, texture, shape, form and space in two or three dimensions. (CD)

ASSESSMENT
Can the children differentiate between subtle shades of one colour?

Beautiful blossom

What you need

The rhyme 'Apple, plum, peach, pear' on page 90; branch of blossom from an apple or another blossom tree; six light twigs about 25cm long; adhesive tape; piece of background paper (approximate size A4) in a soft shade for each child; three or four pots of paints ready-mixed in white and shades of pink; saucer for each paint colour; damp cloth.

Preparation

Fix a twig in the middle of each sheet of paper with two pieces of adhesive tape.

What to do

Say the rhyme 'Apple, plum, peach, pear' with the children. Show the children the real blossom and point out how the blossom grows in different shades of the same colour. Pour some paint out of each pot into a saucer. Invite the children to dip their fingertip into the paint and then gently press it onto the paper, either side of the twig, to create 'finger-print' blossom. When the paint on their finger has been used up they can wipe their finger on the damp cloth and then dip it into another shade of paint. Let them also try using their thumbs to print.

Discussion

The flowers on fruit trees are called blossom. Can the children think of the names of some of these fruit trees? (Apple, plum, peach, pear.) Blossom is very delicate and falls easily off tree branches in a strong wind. When lots of pale pink and white blossom floats down from the trees what does it look like? When the blossom has fallen the tree starts to grow fruit.

Follow-up activities
- Arrange the children's blossom branches all together to make a blossoming tree.
- Find a catkin and stick it on to a small outline drawing of a squirrel. It will look like a furry tail.
- Count how many clusters of blossom there are on one branch of a fruit tree.
- Orange blossom grows in hot countries such as Israel and South Africa. Find these places on a map of the world.

Differentiation

Help younger or less able children to dab a small amount of paint onto their finger to make the prints. Encourage older or more able children to mix some paint colours.

ON THE CD-ROM
- Poem 'Apple, plum, peach, pear'

themes for early years

STEPPING STONE
Show awareness of rhyme and alliteration.

EARLY LEARNING GOAL
Hear and say initial and final sounds in words, and short vowel sounds within words. (CLL)

ASSESSMENT
Do the children show awareness of rhyme and alliteration?

Lazy daisy

What you need
List of riddles describing wild flowering plants (see below); pictures of wild flowers as given in the riddles.

Preparation
Compile a list of riddles similar to the ones given below:
> I'm thinking of a flower which rhymes with lazy, it grows in the grass because it's a ... (Daisy)
> On the edge of the wood there's a lovely smell, everywhere I look there's another ... (Bluebell)
> It starts with an 'r' as everyone knows, it feels very prickly because it's a ... (Rose)
> Two children were lost called Hansel and Gretel, I hope they weren't stung by a stinging ... (Nettle)
> Its purple leaves are as light as a feather, it brings good luck and its name is ... (Heather)

What to do
Show the children the pictures of wild flowers. Read out the riddles and challenge them to guess the answers.

Discussion
Can the children suggest places where weeds would not be welcome? Talk about why don't farmers like weeds. Discuss why we are not supposed to pick some wild flowers. Explain that daisies are weeds that grow in lawns and can be picked. When they have been cut by the lawnmower a few times they learn to grow their flowers on shorter stems so that they won't be chopped off!

Follow-up activities
- Make daisy chains together.
- Make a daisy chain display (see page 78).
- Dye some wild grass by standing it in a jar of warm water, coloured with food dye.
- Use fluted pastry cutters on pieces of thin sliced bread to make flowers you can eat. Spread these shapes with different coloured jams or honey.
- Sing and play 'In and Out the Dusty Bluebells' from *Oranges and Lemons* compiled by Karen King (OUP).
- Say the action poem 'Daisy chain' on page 88.

Differentiation
Help younger or less able children by saying the initial letter of each flower in the rhyme, for example 'd' for 'daisy, 'b' for 'bluebell'. Help older or more able children to read the poem aloud.

ON THE CD-ROM
- Photograph of wild flowers
- Poem 'Daisy chain'

themes for early years

STEPPING STONE
Manipulate materials to achieve a planned effect.

EARLY LEARNING GOAL
Handle tools, objects, construction and malleable materials safely and with increasing control. (PD)

ASSESSMENT
Do the children show patience and interest in planning for a purpose?

My own garden

What you need
Plastic or polystyrene food trays or vegetable punnets from the greengrocer at least 4cm deep (one for each child); pencils; writing paper; scissors; bucket of small washed pebbles (these are cheaper if bought unwashed from a builders' merchant); all-purpose compost; foil plates; grass seed; packet of common thyme seeds; play people; toy garden swings and animals; water container with a spray attachment.

What to do
Tell the children they are going to make their own mini-garden. Ask them to think of how they want to divide their garden and then to draw a plan of it on paper. They should put a layer of pebbles (for drainage) in the base of their container. Cover the pebbles with compost and press it down gently (with a flat hand) so that it comes to just under the rim. They can use the end of a pencil to mark out their planned areas in the compost then water it.

Cut and position some foil (from a foil plate) for a pond, if wanted. Lay down some pebbles for paths. Sow the grass and thyme seeds in the appropriate areas and cover lightly with a thin layer of compost.

Put the mini-garden in a transparent polythene bag and leave it in a warm, light place. In about five days, when the smallest seedlings will have grown to a height of one centimetre, remove the plastic bag.

Arrange the garden toys, people and animals in position. Spray the garden with water frequently to keep it moist. Do not let it become too wet.

Discussion
Talk about the different areas that can be created in a park or garden, for example, flowerbeds, a vegetable patch, lawn, a play area, a pond, paths, sheds, patio, decking, rockery. Talk about how people without gardens can still enjoy growing on a small scale using window boxes, hanging baskets or pots on a balcony.

Follow-up activities
- Show the children the photograph on the CD-ROM titled 'Allotment' to stimulate further discussion.
- Use scissors to cut the grass in your mini-garden.
- Make an instant garden by 'planting' twigs, leaves and flowers into some damp earth or in a tray of damp sand.
- Go for a supervised walk in a residential area to observe the variety of front garden designs.

Differentiation
Use a calendar to help younger children to understand how many days they might need to wait before they see the results of their work. Encourage older or more able children to record how many days the plants take to grow.

ON THE CD-ROM
- Photograph of an allotment

Natural discovery

A beautiful bouquet

STEPPING STONE
Understand that equipment and tools have to be used safely.

EARLY LEARNING GOAL
Handle tools, objects, construction and malleable materials safely and with increasing control. (PD)

ASSESSMENT
Do the children understand that equipment and tools have to be used safely?

What you need
The photocopiable sheet 'Planting instructions' on page 53; soil; planting tools (trowel, small fork, dibber or old pencil, watering can); containers (plastic patio pots, hanging baskets or window boxes); easy-to-grow flower seeds or small flowering plants.

What to do
Invite the children to sequence a set of pictures showing a plant during various stages of growth using the CD-ROM activity titled 'How a plant grows'. Look at the pictures on the photocopiable page 'Planting instructions' with the children. Encourage each child to collect the tools and materials required to plant some seeds or small plants in a pot, hanging basket or window box. Help the children to follow the instructions carefully. Encourage them to care for their plants by watering them regularly, removing weeds and checking for pests such as greenfly.

Discussion
Talk with the children about their experience or desires regarding planting flowers. Talk about familiar and less familiar gardening tools and their uses, for example, spades and trowels are used to dig the earth; forks are used to break up large lumps of soil; a dibber is like a pencil and is used to make holes in the soil to plant seedlings. Talk about why a watering can or hose is so important. Discuss what might happen if plants where not watered regularly in hot weather.

Follow-up activities
- Invite the children to push some dried soil through a garden sieve to make it fine enough for planting tiny seeds.
- Help the children sow seeds randomly in a flowerbed outside.
- Help the children sow seeds in a straight row using garden canes or string as a guideline along the ground.
- Sing the song 'Grandad loves his garden' on page 80.
- Look at the photograph of an allotment on the CD-ROM.

Differentiation
Invite younger or less able children to work in pairs. Encourage older or more able children to write the name of the seeds or flowers on a flat wooden stick to identify each plant.

ON THE CD-ROM
- On-screen activity 'How a plant grows'
- Photocopiable sheet 'Planting instructions'
- Photograph of an allotment
- Song 'Grandad loves his garden'

Planting instructions

● Follow these steps to plant seeds or small plants in pots, window boxes or baskets.

pebbles

soil

seeds or plants

water

sunshine

enjoy

Growing our food

In this chapter the children are given the opportunity to handle a variety of food and learn about the different places where it has been grown.

Tell the story

Stories and rhymes

themes for early years

STEPPING STONE
Introduce a story or narrative into their play.

EARLY LEARNING GOAL
Use their imagination in art and design, music, dance, imaginative and role play and stories. (CD)

ASSESSMENT
Are the children keen to use their imagination for creating role-play scenarios and stories?

What you need
The photocopiable sheet 'The enormous strawberry' on page 55; the traditional story 'The Enormous Turnip' (Ladybird Books); child scissors; coloured pens.

What to do
Read the traditional story of 'The Enormous Turnip' to the children. Provide each child with a copy of the photocopiable sheet 'The enormous strawberry' and ask them to compare the pictures in the storybook with the scenes depicted here.

Invite the children to colour in and cut out the four pictures on the sheet and to arrange them in order. Encourage them to use the pictures to tell an adapted version of the turnip story. Help the children to think of a title for their 'new' story or play, for example, 'The Gigantic Strawberry' or 'The Biggest Strawberry Ever Seen'!

Discussion
Talk about where different fruits and vegetables grow, for example, above ground or underground; on trees or on bushes? Look together at the pictures showing the turnip and strawberry in the book and on the photocopiable sheet. Ask questions such as: *Does a turnip grow above ground or in the soil? Where does a strawberry grow?* Talk about the term 'root vegetable'. Can the children name some common root vegetables?

> **Follow-up activities**
> ● Wear a blindfold and play a game of tasting fruit and guessing what it is.
> ● Make some clay fruit or vegetables and paint them.
> ● Use a squeezer to make some fresh orange juice or a blender (with adult supervision) to make a fruit or vegetable smoothie.

Differentiation
Provide younger children with simple props to inspire role plays, such as a red cushion to represent a strawberry, dressing-up clothes for the characters and so on. Encourage older or more able children to add imaginary details to their story, for example, the name and age of the characters, the time of year, where they all live and so on.

ON THE CD-ROM
● Photocopiable sheet 'The enormous strawberry'

The enormous strawberry

● Use the pictures to retell the story.

Food

themes for early years

STEPPING STONE
Extend vocabulary, especially by grouping and naming.

EARLY LEARNING GOAL
Extend their vocabulary, exploring the meanings and sounds of new words. (CLL)

ASSESSMENT
Do the children listen and respond to 'new' words and are they interested in exploring the meanings and sounds of 'new' words?

Let's compare

What you need
Two card copies of the photocopiable sheet 'Veggie snap' on page 57; pens or pencils in shades of orange, purple, yellow, green, red and brown; child scissors; examples of: carrot, beetroot, yellow pepper, green beans, radish, potato.

What to do
Display the six vegetables for the children to observe, handle, discuss and compare. Ask the children to name and identify the vegetables and talk about the variety of different shapes, textures and colours. Encourage descriptive language, such as, 'smooth', 'rough', 'bumpy', 'ridges', 'shiny' and introduce new descriptive words as appropriate.

Provide the children with two copies of the photocopiable sheet 'Veggie snap' to colour in, using the real vegetables and the word labels as a guide. Help the children to cut out the twelve pictures to create a set of playing cards for games such as Pairs and Snap.

Discussion
Do the children know the names of any other vegetables? In this country vegetables such as green beans will only grow in the summer when the weather is really warm. What makes it possible for us to have vegetables such as peas and green beans in the colder months of winter? (Peas, for example, can be frozen, dried or tinned.) Which other vegetables will grow only in the summer? Some vegetables, such as swedes, can be grown in the cold winter months because the main part of them grows under the soil where it is warmer.

Follow-up activities
● Display a selection of other real vegetables for the children to observe, sort, handle and compare.
● Invite the children to make an additional set of twelve playing cards by drawing pictures of other vegetables of similar colour onto squares of blank card. (For example, green peas, orange marrow, red cabbage, purple aubergine and yellow corn.)
● Ask the children to look out for white or cream coloured vegetables while at home or out shopping, for example, cauliflower, cooked potato, haricot beans and white cabbage. Alternatively, arrange a display of white vegetables in your setting for the children to name and identify.
● Tell the traditional stories of 'The Princess and the Pea' or 'Jack and the Beanstalk' (Ladybird Books).

Differentiation
Help younger or less able children by introducing descriptive terms and by explaining what the 'new' words mean. Challenge older or more able children to describe a vegetable for their peers to identify.

ON THE CD-ROM
● Photocopiable sheet 'Veggie snap'

Veggie snap

● Make two or more copies to cut out and colour.

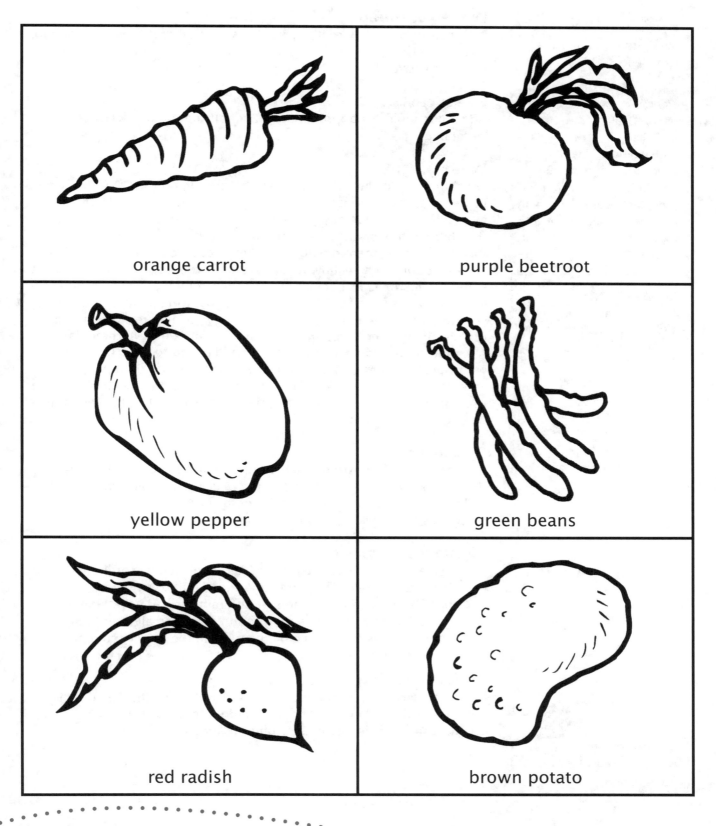

orange carrot

purple beetroot

yellow pepper

green beans

red radish

brown potato

Food

themes for early years

Vegetable forests

What you need
Selection of fresh raw root vegetables such as carrots, swede, parsnip, turnip, beetroot; chopping board; vegetable knife (adult use only); shallow plastic dishes.

Preparation
An adult should cut approximately 2cm off the top of each root vegetable.

What to do
Encourage the children to view the photograph on the CD-ROM to inspire discussion about growing plants and vegetables at home or in an allotment. Have any of them grown vegetables at home? Invite the children to work as a team to grow and care for a mini 'vegetable forest'! Begin by encouraging the children to place an assortment of vegetable tops in a shallow dish, cut side down. Invite them to scatter some small stones or pebbles around the vegetable tops to create an interesting base and to pour a little water over the pebbles, making sure that the vegetables are not completely covered in water. Place the dish in a sunny position, indoors, for approximately three days. Ask the children to check the dish every day and to keep it topped up with water. Encourage them to get together to share thoughts, views and ideas about what will happen to the vegetable tops? Gradually the vegetable tops will grow, creating the appearance of lush, green forest trees growing on mini islands!

Discussion
Ask the children questions such as: *Which vegetable top grew the highest, the widest, the darkest or the thickest?* Discuss what would make the forest scene look more wild, for example, toy sharks or crocodiles in the water, or dinosaurs on the islands.

Follow-up activities
● Make a collection of vegetables and sort them according to those that grow above the ground and those that grow below.
● Make a chart using pictures of different-shaped vegetables. Label the columns: 'long ones', 'big round ones', 'small round ones', 'other shapes', and place the pictures in the correct column.

Differentiation
Help younger children to keep the dish topped up with the correct quantity of water. Encourage older children to make a daily record of growth using words, pictures or photographs.

ON THE CD-ROM
● Photograph showing herbs in pots

Sound

Snap, crackle and pop

themes for early years

STEPPING STONE
Tap out simple repeated rhythms and make some up.

EARLY LEARNING GOAL
Recognise and explore how sounds can be changed, sing simple songs from memory, recognise repeated sounds and sound patterns and match movements to music. (CD)

ASSESSMENT
Do the children enjoy tapping out sounds and are they willing to attempt making up simple repeated rhythms?

What you need
A collection of objects that can be used to make sound, for example: a chain, a wooden spoon, a comb, bubble wrap, a plastic bottle, an empty plastic tub, scrap paper, metal spoons and so on.

What to do
Invite the children to join in making up repeated sounds and rhythms using their voices, their hands and feet and a collection of suitable objects while listening to the words in a harvest-themed story. For example:

Mr Farmer starts up his tractor (*thud, rattle, rumble*). The machinery spins (*clank, rattle, clatter*) and rakes through the soil to scatter the seeds. The crows squawk (*caw caw*) and the mice scurry (*scratch, scratch)* around for spare seeds. As the shoots start to grow, the rabbits and hares hop across the ground (*boing, boing)* to eat them. The rain falls (*tap, pitter, patter*) and waters the shoots that grow tall in the bright warm sun. The corn sways in the breeze (*swish, whoosh*) and Mr Farmer climbs up into his combine harvester *(stomp, stamp)* to start the harvest (*brume, rumble, hum*).

Discussion
How did the children make the sound of the tractor? Which was their favourite sound effect? How many different sounds did they create? Talk about harvest time and ask the children to share their memory and experience of seasonal festivals and celebrations.

Follow-up activities
- Invite the children to perform their harvest story, with sound effects, during a seasonal festival at your setting.
- Tape-record the story, with the children's sound effects, for them to listen to and discuss with their peers.
- Sing and play 'The Farmer's in his Den' from *Oranges and Lemons* compiled by Karen King (OUP). Invite the children to tap out sounds and rhythms to accompany the song.
- Say the poem 'The farmer knows' on page 93.

Differentiation
Familiarise younger children with the story before inviting them to make up the sounds and rhythms. Encourage older or more able children to make up their own harvest-themed story.

ON THE CD-ROM
- Poem 'The farmer knows'

Construction and malleable materials

Dingle, dangle scarecrow

What you need
For each child: A4 paper; paper circle; paper rectangle; wooden lolly stick; twig about 18cm in length; 'T' shaped felt to use for the hat; straw or string; small gummed shapes such as squares, ovals or triangles; adhesive tape; glue; felt-tipped pens; the song 'Dingle, dangle scarecrow' on page 79.

What to do
Sing the song 'Dingle, dangle scarecrow' with the children and invite them to join in making a scarecrow picture. Help the children to describe, name and identify the shapes they are going to use. Help them to tape the twig in place across the middle of the A4 paper, for the scarecrow's arms, and to tape the lolly stick just below these arms. They can stick the oblong 'body' over the top of the tape and the stick (see illustration). Ask the children to stick the circle onto the body and to glue some straw on the top of his head before they glue the hat on at a jaunty angle. Encourage them to decorate the scarecrow by using a selection of small paper shapes to create a colourful jacket, and to draw in the scarecrows face using felt-tipped pens.

Discussion
What shapes did you use to decorate the scarecrow's jacket? What other shapes could you use to make his body, hat and face? (For example, triangles, ovals, squares, pentagons and hexagons.) Which shapes have four sides? Which shapes have three corners?

Follow-up activities
● Help the children to make a 3D model of a scarecrow using materials such as cardboard boxes, card tubes and sponge ball spheres and so on.
● Use art straws to make geometric shapes then count how many sides and corners each shape has.

Differentiation
Help younger children to name the different shapes. Encourage older or more able children to cut out their own shapes for making the scarecrow.

Role play

Supermarkets

themes for early years

STEPPING STONE
Use mathematical language in play.

EARLY LEARNING GOAL
Use developing mathematical ideas and methods to solve practical problems. (MD)

ASSESSMENT
Are the children able to use mathematical language in play, for example, one more, two less, add, take away, how much?

What you need
Selection of clean and empty food packets, boxes, yoghurt pots, plastic bottles and cartons; small world toys (such as, plastic food, fruit and vegetables, shopping baskets, carrier bags, toy till); real or pretend money; torch to use as a bar code scanner; scales; carrier bags; small sticky labels; pens.

What to do
Position tables in the role-play area to make 'shopping aisles'. Lay out the goods on the tables. Set up a chair and table for the checkout and arrange the scales, scanner, till, money and carrier bags nearby.

Help the children to write pretend price labels for the goods on display and invite them to take it in turns to be a customer, a checkout assistant, shelf filler or a manager. Encourage them to use the props, money and price labels for role-play scenarios that involve practical problem-solving skills such as buying and selling, or adding prices and working out change.

Discussion
Use the role-play scenarios to inspire discussion about where our food and drink comes from. Help the children to check the labels on the pots, boxes and bottles for the countries where the food or ingredients were grown. Do they realise that some foods are grown abroad? Use a map of the world to identify the countries where the food originated. Explain that bananas grow in bunches in countries which have plenty of water and heat. Ask why oranges and lemons grow on trees in hot places such as Israel and Spain but not in this country. Explain that sugar cane grows well in India and Cuba which are hot, wet countries. Rice likes hot and steamy weather and begins growing under mud in the paddy fields of countries like India and China. Ask the children if they have lived in, or visited any of these places. If so what can they recall?

Follow-up activities
- Cut out pictures of food from magazines and stick them on to the giant outline of a supermarket trolley.
- Talk about what shopping was like before there were supermarkets.
- Sing the song 'Our food' on page 81.

Differentiation
Help younger or less able children to label foods with prices between 1p and 10p. Encourage older or more able children to label foods with prices up to 50p or more.

ON THE CD-ROM
- Song 'Our food'

Construction and malleable materials

themes for early years

Harvest time

What you need
A3 card copies of the photocopiable sheet 'Apple bingo' on page 63; counters or buttons; scissors; 26 blank playing cards or plain paper; pens.

What to do
Talk to the children about harvest time and invite them to help construct the components for a simple harvest-themed game called 'Apple bingo'. Help the children to cut the photocopiable sheet into sections to create a set of six 'Apple bowl' gameboards. Help the children to label 26 playing cards with the letters of the alphabet. Play the games as follows:

Place the letter cards face down. Provide each child with a gameboard and help them to say the letters in the apple shapes. Give each child six counters and explain that you are going to reveal one letter card at a time. If they have the same letter on their game board, they should cover it with a counter. When they have covered all the apples on their game board they can call out *Bingo*. The children can then play the game again using a different gameboard.

Discussion
Use the game to inspire an interest in harvest-time traditions. Christians decorate their churches with fruit, flowers, vegetables and loaves of bread. Jewish people build a little shelter that has fruit and vegetables hanging from the roof, for a week they eat all their meals in this shelter called a 'Sukkah'. Hindus sing, dance and feast to celebrate their harvest festival called 'Baisaki'. Buddhists have a 'first fruit' ceremony when they offer Buddha a large bowl of milk and rice. Ask the children to talk about festivals and traditions that they have enjoyed with family and friends.

Follow-up activities
● If possible invite parents, carers and grandparents into your setting to talk with the children about their favourite celebrations.
● Arrange a harvest display in your setting.
● Act out the poem 'The crop song' on page 94.

Differentiation
Sit with younger or less able children during the game. Encourage older or more able children to take it in turns to reveal the letter cards.

ON THE CD-ROM
● Photocopiable sheet 'Apple bingo'
● Poem 'The crop song'

Apple bingo

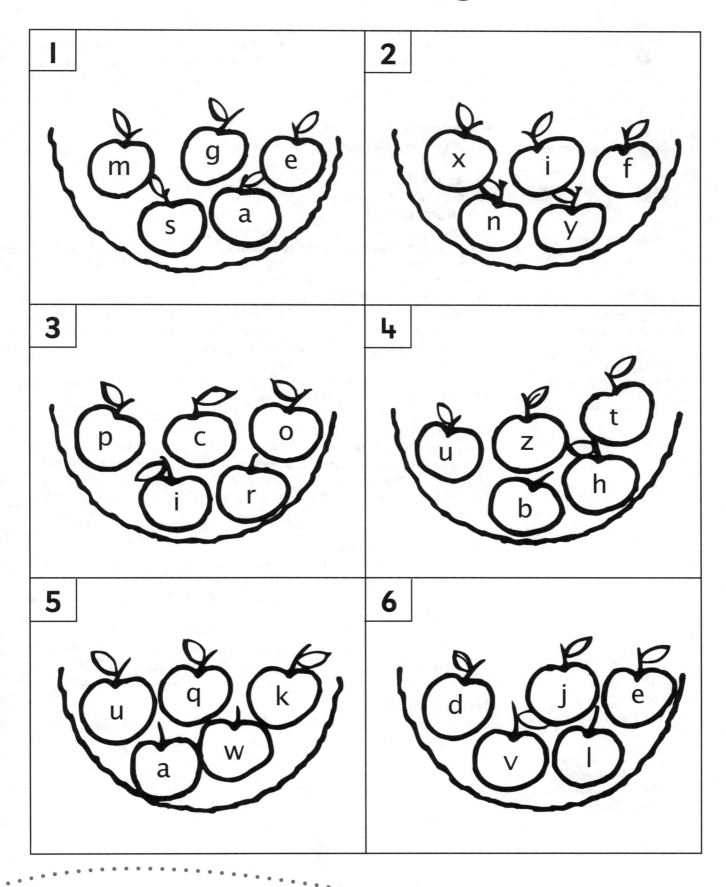

Food

themes for early years

Watch it rise!

What you need
The photocopiable sheet 'How to make bread' on page 65; large bowl; small bowl; floured board; buttered baking tray; ingredients listed on photocopiable page 65; oven (for adult use only); hand-washing facilities; clean aprons.

Preparation
Check for food allergies and dietary requirements.

What to do
Ask the children to wash their hands and to wear an apron. Show them the photocopiable recipe page and ask them to help follow the instructions, step by step. Encourage the children to press, squeeze and poke the dough as they knead it for ten minutes on a floured board. Cover the dough for approximately 30 minutes to let it rise. Encourage the children to peep under the cloth, at intervals, so they can see it grow higher and wider. When the dough has risen, invite the children to repeat the kneading stage, then help them to divide the dough into small rolls. Leave the rolls to rise for another 30 minutes. Once again, encourage the children to keep peeping at the dough to see the rolls grow bigger! An adult should bake the rolls and then leave them to cool on a wire rack. Invite the children to taste the rolls with butter or let them take the rolls home to share with their family.

Discussion
Encourage the children to describe what they did and what they saw during the activity. Ask them to use their hands to show how the dough changed as it grew bigger under the cloth. Which part of the activity did the children enjoy most, the mixing, the kneading, the watching or the eating?

Follow-up activities
● Make up two bread mixtures (one with yeast, the other without). Compare their sizes after leaving them both covered in a warm place for approximately 30 minutes. Which dough has risen and why?
● Invite the children to draw or paint pictures showing the method they used to make the bread rolls. Display the pictures on the wall to inspire discussion about growth and change.

Differentiation
Help younger or less able children to wash their hands properly before handling the food. Encourage older or more able children to weigh out the ingredients.

How to make bread

Ingredients

575g sifted plain flour
1 tsp salt
1 tsp caster sugar
12g butter
25g fresh yeast
300ml warm water
150ml warm milk

A large bowl

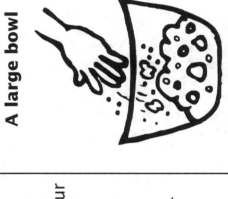

Put flour, salt and sugar into a bowl. Rub in the butter.

A small bowl

Mix yeast with some warm water until creamy.

The large bowl

Mix the creamy yeast, warm milk and warm water with the dry ingredients to create a firm dough.

Floured board

Knead for about ten minutes.

Floured board

Cover and leave to rise for 30 minutes.

Floured board

Knead again and divide into small rolls.

Buttered baking tray

Leave rolls to rise for 30 minutes. Then bake at 230°C/450°F/Gas 8 for 20 minutes.

Before the advance of technology plants provided the raw materials for making things. This chapter shows some of the ways in which plants can be used in our everyday lives.

Lavender's blue

themes for early years

STEPPING STONE
Value and contribute to own well-being and self-control.

EARLY LEARNING GOAL
Work as part of a group or class, taking turns and sharing fairly, understanding that there needs to be agreed values and codes of behaviour for groups of people, including adults and children, to work together harmoniously. (PSED)

ASSESSMENT
Do the children work as part of a group or class, taking turns and sharing fairly?

What you need
Dishcloths (trim each cloth to create two squares); dried lavender flower heads; tablespoon; rubber bands, ribbon or thick wool.

What to do
Let the children take it in turns to handle and smell the lavender. Ask them to work in pairs to measure one level tablespoon of lavender to put into the middle of each dishcloth square. They should then carefully gather up the corners of the cloth to form a small pouch, and help each other secure the pouch with a rubber band. Ask them to work together to cut and tie a length of ribbon or wool around the neck of the bag. Help the children tie the ribbon into a pretty bow or loop for hanging.

Discussion
How many different herbs can the children see in the photograph on the CD-ROM? What colour and shape are the leaves? Can the children see a lavender plant? Lavender is evergreen. Help the children to use information books to find out if all herbs are evergreen. Lavender produces blue or mauve flowers. Do other herbs produce flowers? Lavender has a very sweet smell which bees and butterflies love. Do other herbs have distinctive smells? Talk about why a herb garden might be a wonderful place for a blind person to visit.

Follow-up activities
● Try making another sachet using dried rosemary or thyme.
● Sing the nursery rhyme 'Lavender's Blue Dilly Dilly' from *The Kingfisher Nursery Collection* (Kingfisher).
● Mix dried herbs, dried flower petals and lemon or orange peel. Put this pot-pourri into a pot with a tight-fitting lid. To freshen your room and make it smell sweet, open the pot and shake gently.

Differentiation
Encourage younger or less able children to work in pairs. Encourage older children to act as group helpers by selecting the appropriate tools, trimming the materials and clearing away.

ON THE CD-ROM
● Photograph of herbs in pots

Construction
and malleable
materials

themes for early years

Three little pigs

What you need
A copy of the story 'The Three Little Pigs' (Traditional); straw (or a bag of hay from a pet shop); twigs or sticks (or garden cane from a garden centre); Plasticine; plastic or wooden construction bricks.

What to do
Read or tell the children the story of 'The Three Little Pigs'. Show them the materials you have provided and plan with them how they could make houses like those the little pigs made. Let the children work in pairs and allow each pair a chance to use the straw, sticks and bricks to build their model houses. If they run into difficulties you could suggest that they hollow out the straw like a nest. If the sticks will not stay up recommend that one stick is pushed into a Plasticine 'dome' to serve as a central pole and the other sticks can meet it at the top to make a cone shape. To make the brick house sturdy, the children will need to build with the bricks in a staggered fashion. When they have finished, invite them to test the strength of their buildings by blowing, pushing or knocking them.

Discussion
Which of the buildings was the strongest? The first types of houses that people built were made of mud, grass, bark and twigs. These weren't strong enough to cope with bad weather so people started using bricks to build their homes. Bricks are still used today for many different types of building. What sort of brick buildings can the children see near to your setting? Are there any buildings nearby that have been made using other materials, for example, thatch for the roof, wood cladding, glass walls and so on? There are many different types of homes. What kind of house do the children live in?

Follow-up activities
● Make a list of all the things that would be needed to build a house: wood, nails, floorboards, roof tiles and windows.
● Use construction straws to make the framework for different-shaped houses.
● What are the names of the homes of pigs, horses, birds, mice (and other animals)?
● Sing the song 'The three little pigs' on page 84.

Differentiation
Help younger or less able children by providing hands-on assistance. Encourage older or more able children to use trial and error during the construction stage.

themes for early years

Rings and balls

STEPPING STONE
Retrieve, collect and catch objects.

EARLY LEARNING GOAL
Use a range of small and large equipment. (PD)

ASSESSMENT
Are the children able to retrieve, collect and catch objects with increasing control?

What you need
An assortment of large, medium and small rubber balls including tennis balls; six rubber quoits; six empty plastic drinks bottles; gravel or sand; empty bucket; house brick; rubber safety mat.

Preparation
Fill three of the plastic bottles with gravel or sand and screw on the lids tightly. Set up the circuit of small games equipment as illustrated.

What to do
Explain to the children that they are all going to take turns to stop and play at each 'station' of the circuit. Demonstrate how to use each piece of equipment. At Station 1, they will throw the hoops over the bottles; at 2, bounce the big balls with the flat of their hand; at 3, they will kneel about two metres away from a partner and roll the ball across the floor to each other; at 4, they will knock over as many bottles as they can with one roll of the ball; at 5, throw the balls into the bucket that is leaning on the brick; at 6, they will do a somersault on the mat. Make sure that the children tuck their heads in well here, before pushing off with their feet. Warn them of the dangers of throwing balls too high or too hard.

1.  2.

3.  4.

5.  6.

Discussion
Balls, quoits and safety mats are bouncy and are made of rubber. What else is made of rubber? (Erasers, balloons.) When a hole is made in the bark of a rubber tree a milk-like liquid flows out. This sticky gum is used to make rubber. Rubber stretches and is used in elastic to keep up socks and trousers, and to make rubber bands and bouncy castles. Rubber is waterproof and is used to make raincoats. Which other waterproof things are made of rubber? (Rubber gloves, boats, flippers.) Bicycle tyres and car tyres need to be strong, flexible and waterproof – they are also made of rubber.

Follow-up activities
● Use the photocopiable sheet 'Playing the game' on page 69 and draw lines to match ball to bucket, shuttlecock to bat, ring to stand and child to hoop. How many are left over in each picture?
● Nip the top leaf off a rubber plant and watch the gum flow.
● Test different fabrics to see if they are waterproof (include rubber gloves and wellington boots).

Differentiation
Offer verbal encouragement to boost the confidence of younger or less able children. Encourage more able children to help set up the circuit.

ON THE CD-ROM
● Photocopiable sheet 'Playing the game'

Playing the game

● Draw lines to match the games equipment.

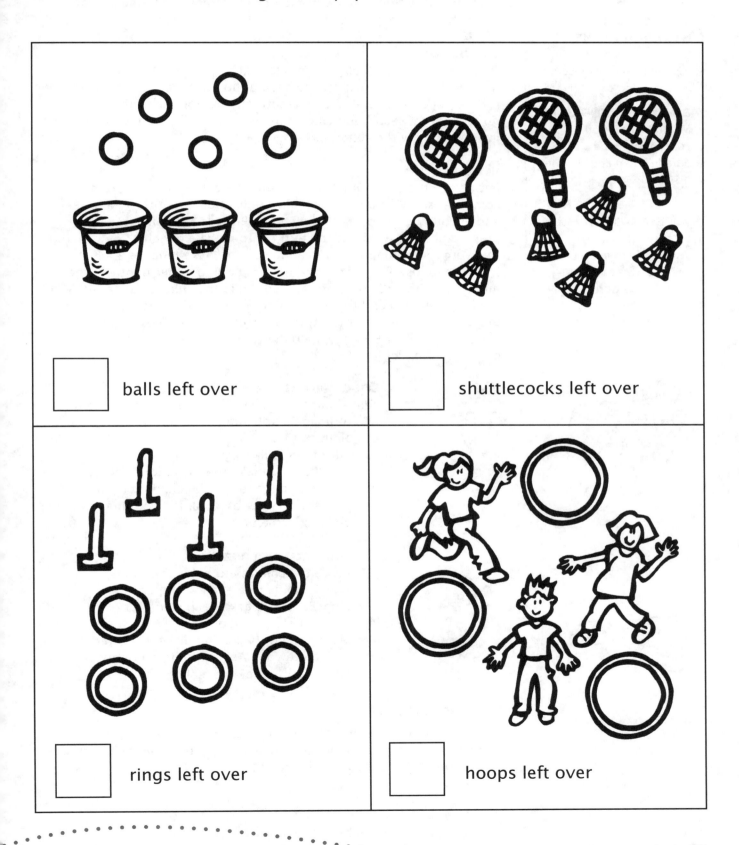

balls left over

shuttlecocks left over

rings left over

hoops left over

Art and craft

themes for early years

Easter chick

What you need
Thick yellow wool; straight-backed chair; scraps of orange and black card; child scissors; glue stick; access to the internet.

Preparation
To prepare separate balls of wool for each child, wind wool from the main ball round the back of the chair about 16 times, cut it off and then roll it up. Cut a separate 20cm length of wool for each child. In advance do an internet search for 'chick hatching' to find a suitable film clip, or image, to show the children.

What to do
Encourage the children to observe the film clip, or image, on the computer showing a chick hatching. Talk about what they have seen and encourage them to ask questions. Provide the children with a prepared ball of wool and invite them to make a toy chick by winding the wool round their four spread fingers to make loops (see illustration). Slide the loops off their fingers and tie them together tightly in the middle with the 20cm length of wool. Help the children to carefully cut the loops at each end to create the fluffy body of a chick. Invite them to make a beak and eyes by cutting out a diamond shape and two circles from coloured card. Finally, help the children to glue the beak and eyes onto their woollen chick.

STEPPING STONE
Show increasing independence in selecting and carrying out activities.

EARLY LEARNING GOAL
Maintain attention, concentrate, and sit quietly when appropriate. (PSED)

ASSESSMENT
Do the children listen attentively to instructions and are they able to concentrate during each stage of the activity?

Discussion
Talk about the appearance of the chick in the film clip or image. Explain that when a chick first hatches out of an egg its feathers are damp and straggly, but soon dry to look like a yellow fluffy ball. Observe the wool used to make the toy chick. Discuss where wool comes from and ask the children to think of things that are made of wool, for example, jumpers, carpets and blankets.

Follow-up activities
● Invite the children to help make a display of woolly items to feel and compare.
● Sing 'Baa Baa Black Sheep' and 'Mary Had a Little Lamb' (Traditional).
● Make a 'feely' bag using different materials including wool. Ask the children to guess which fabric they are feeling.

Differentiation
Help younger or less able children to wrap the wool around a strip of stiff card instead of their fingers. Encourage older or more able children to help prepare the wool for the activity.

Water

themes for early years

Mashed paper

What you need
Ten large sheets of newspaper (20 if tabloid size); washing-up bowl; litre of water; 50g flour; dinner plate; pot of mixed orange paint; paint brushes; PVA adhesive; the poem 'Save our trees' on page 95.

What to do
Tear the sheets of newspaper up into small pieces. Put them into the bowl and pour the water over them. Make sure that all the paper is wet. Leave it to stand for a couple of hours until most of the water has been absorbed. Pour off any excess water and sprinkle on the flour. Let the children stand around the bowl and squeeze and knead the mixture with their hands until it is thoroughly mashed. They can then take a handful of the pulp each and, with two hands, form it into a ball about the size of a tangerine. Leave the balls on the plate for about five days until they have dried out completely. Paint them orange and when dry glaze them with diluted PVA adhesive, which will turn transparent when dry.

Discussion
Read the poem 'Save our trees' and talk with the children about what the rhyme means. Explain that paper is made from trees. Once the tree has been cut down its wood is broken up into very small pieces and mixed to a pulp with water. It is spread out flat and pressed till all the water is squeezed out and then left to dry. Because we use paper for so many things we cut down far too many trees. How can we all help to prevent so many trees from being cut down?

Follow-up activities
● Plant a tree with the children and talk about why planting trees is important.
● Make a display of household objects labelled 'Made from recycled materials', for example, certain types of writing paper and celebration cards, some disposal bags and toilet paper and a variety of packaging.
● Find out where the local recycling points are and identify the materials that are collected for recycling.

Differentiation
Help younger or less able children to form the pulp into a firm ball. Encourage older or more able children to use the pulp to model a variety of different fruit shapes.

ON THE CD-ROM
● Poem 'Save our trees'

themes for early years

STEPPING STONE
Use one object to represent another, even when the objects have few characteristics in common.

EARLY LEARNING GOAL
Use their imagination in art and design, music, dance, imaginative and role play and stories. (CD)

ASSESSMENT
Are the children willing and able to use their imagination in art?

Trailing display

What you need
Bottle corks; colourful poster (or acrylic) paints; sponges; trays or tubs; display board; wavy-cut strips of plain paper or fabric (approximate size 10cm × 30cm); green felt-tipped pens (or green paint and fine paint brushes); glue or a child safe stapler.

What to do
Place several small sponges in shallow pots or trays and help the children to dampen the sponges with different-coloured paints. Encourage the children to press the circular cork ends into the dampened sponges to create colourful printing tools. Invite them to use the paint soaked corks to print a row of fantasy flower shapes across several long, narrow strips of paper or fabric. Encourage the children to use their creative imagination to produce a variety of different floral shapes and patterns. When these are dry, provide the children with a green felt-tipped pen (or paintbrush) to link the row of printed flowers using elaborate wavy lines to represent entwined stems and vines curling between the flower heads. Secure a semi-circle of brown paper onto the top half of the display board to represent a basket. Help the children to glue or staple several floral strips across the rim of the 'basket' so they hang down freely, creating the effect of beautiful trailing flowers.

Discussion
Explain that cork is a very useful material. Cork is the bark of an evergreen oak tree. Look carefully at the little holes in a cork; these holes are the pores through which the tree bark used to breathe. Air gets trapped in these pores, which helps to make cork light enough to float on water. Encourage the children to try floating the corks when they have finished printing. Talk about how useful wood and cork are in our everyday lives.

Follow-up activities
● Make a display of things made from cork and wood.
● Experiment making boats to float in the water tray using bottle corks and different types of wood.

Differentiation
Show younger or less able children how to print floral patterns using the corks. Encourage older or more able children to use white paint to mix a variety of pastel shades for printing.

themes for early years

T-shirts

STEPPING STONE
Match some shapes by recognising similarities and orientation.

EARLY LEARNING GOAL
Talk about, recognise and recreate simple patterns. (MD)

ASSESSMENT
Have the children gained the confidence to talk about and recognise simple patterns?

What you need
'T' shape template (see illustration); child scissors; assorted pieces of thin cotton material; glue; background paper; coloured pens and pencils.

Preparation
Use the T-shirt template to cut out several shapes from cotton material.

What to do
Invite the children to use the cotton 'T' shapes to make a pattern on their background paper. If they are happy with their arrangement they can stick the T-shirts into place. When they have finished they can find each rectangle between the T-shirts and write a big 'T' in this space with a coloured pencil or felt-tipped pen. Alternatively, invite the children to write their initial letter in the gap or to design a small pattern, logo or geometric shape.

Discussion
Is anyone in the group wearing a T-shirt today? Why is it called a T-shirt? The shapes used for the pattern are made of cotton, which comes from a growing plant. Cottonseeds are sown in fields, in hot countries, and can grow into plants as tall as a child! When the pods, called bolls, are ripe they burst open and show the seeds, which are held in a mass of soft white fibres. The cotton field looks as if it is covered with lots of fluffy snowballs the size of apples. The cottonseeds are picked and separated from the white fluff. A machine spins the fluff into cotton thread and another machine weaves it into cloth for making clothes. How many things can children think of that are made of cotton?

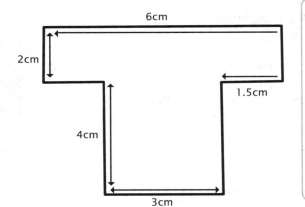

Follow-up activities
● Tie-dye squares of white cotton fabric.
● Children can pencil their initials on a card and punch holes (not too close together) along the line of the letters. Use thick cotton thread to stitch along the outline.
● See how many cotton reels the children can build into a tower before the tower falls over.
● Examine a piece of cotton wool and pull it apart.
● Make a collage using things that grow (see the display 'Things that grow' on page 75).

Differentiation
Help younger or less able children to fit the shapes together. Encourage older or more able children to help prepare for the activity by drawing and cutting the out 'T' shapes.

ICT

themes for early years

String strands

What you need

Six pieces of thick paper or card (about A4 size); thick garden twine from a garden centre (do not use synthetic string); scissors; glue and spreaders; computer with a paint program; colour printer; photograph of a tree in four seasons on the CD-ROM.

What to do

Observe real trees or pictures of trees in winter including the photograph of a tree in four seasons provided on the CD-ROM. Invite the children to use a paint program on the computer to design and create a 'free-style' picture representing a tree with no leaves, a gnarled trunk and interesting branches spreading upwards and outwards. Help the children to print their pictures.

Invite the children to create a second tree picture using a totally different method of design. Let them cut a piece of string that is slightly shorter than the length of their piece of paper. Explain that they are going to use it to make the shape of a tree in winter. Show them how they can unravel the fibres of the string into strands but only undo to just under half way. Each strand can then be teased out with fingernails until it is quite fluffy. Stick the 'trunk' part of the string on to the paper. Don't stick down all the fluffy bits; they will look more realistic if left sticking up. Leave the tree pictures flat until the glue is dry.

Discussion

Compare the computer pictures with the string pictures and talk about the different methods of design and construction. Which method of design do the children enjoy most? Explain that string is thin rope. Many thousands of years ago, rope was made by plaiting grasses together. Can the children think of how many uses there are for rope or string? (Washing line, rope ladder, yo-yo, guy ropes for a tent, pulling a sledge.)

Follow-up activities
- Display the computer-generated tree pictures next to the string pictures to discuss and compare.
- Tie three strands of string to the back of a chair and plait them.
- Dip a piece of string into thick paint then wiggle it over a piece of paper to make a pattern.

Differentiation

Help younger or less able children to operate the computer successfully. Encourage older or more able children to print their picture using different colours or to add a name label using their choice of font.

Displays

Creating colourful, purposeful displays helps to promote an interesting and exciting atmosphere that can play a valuable role in improving the children's learning environment and in promoting enthusiasm for a theme or topic. Displays not only reassure children how much we value their work but also demonstrate skills to parents, carers and visitors.

Setting up and using displays

Use three-dimensional features within a display to create added interest: stick bits of polystyrene or card behind a drawing to 'raise' it; suspend work from the top of the display; limit the stapling so that not everything is completely flat, leaving bits sticking up or out. Using a mixture of mediums such as paper, fabric and natural materials (like grass or twigs) will make the display more lively and varied.

Add purpose to the display by using appropriate labels: bold name labels can help to promote a child's sense of pride in their achievements; captions offer an opportunity for the children to express thoughts and feelings about a picture, photograph or poster; single word labels can be used to encourage an interest in reading. Involve the children in writing name labels, captions or single words, either by hand or using the computer.

Things that grow

What you need

Piece of stiff cardboard; range of materials from growing plants or animals (straw, hay, different types of paper, an old clean woollen sweater or socks, cotton fabric, string); pictures of the plants and animals from which the materials derived; PVA glue; scissors.

What to do

Help the children to cut up the different materials. Encourage them to glue all these pieces randomly, onto the sheet of stiff cardboard. The idea is to cover the top of the card as closely as possible with the different materials. When dry, repeat this process on the other side of the card. The result will be a 3D collage of different colours and textures using all natural materials. As you work together, explain to the children which materials come from growing plants and which come from animals. Observe the pictures of the plants and animals from which the materials derived. Encourage the children to talk about the different textures using descriptive terms such as, *soft, rough, smooth* and *bumpy*. Hang the double sided collage up to create a colourful mobile. Help the children to write labels such as 'straw', 'paper', 'wool', 'cotton' and 'string' onto pieces of card to hang from the mobile.

Pond life

What you need

Black, brown and green tissue and/or crêpe paper; white card; scraps of lace or a doily; scissors; crayons or felt-tipped pens; thick black felt-tipped pens; bubble wrap; black bin bag; adhesive and spreaders; large piece of blue backing paper; staple gun (adult use only).

What to do

Staple the blue background paper to the display area. Make the water plants by tearing narrow strips of green tissue paper. Give the children these strips and show them how to hold one end and twist the other end before fixing these spirals upright onto the background. Make other water weeds by cutting slits along the top edge of a rectangle of green crêpe paper to make a long fringe. Pleat this rectangle, gather it at the bottom and fix the bottom point to the background. It should fan out slightly. The children can screw up some brown tissue paper to serve as underwater rocks and stones. Staple these weeds and stones onto the background. Help the children to draw or paint a frog, a newt and a dragonfly on the white card. Cut them out and let the children stick lace wings on the dragonfly. Fix these and some bubble wrap 'frog-spawn' among the weeds and stones. Cut out small circles of black plastic from the bin bag to make water beetles. Stick these on to the 'pond' and let the children draw the black legs and black tadpole shapes directly on to the background paper.

DISCUSSION

Ponds provide a habitat for a variety of wildlife. What do pond creatures eat? Water plants can grow so much that they nearly choke the pond, leaving no room for the other wildlife. Some plants may need to be removed each year. There is a lot to see, even in a small pond, but it is dangerous for young children to go to watch it on their own.

Growing

Bean sequence

What you need
Growing bean (see 'Roots and shoots' on page 36); cardboard template in the shape of a glass jar (approximate size A5); six pieces of white card (approximate size A4); pencil; felt-tipped pens; brown and green paper; scissors; six paper towels; glue; spreader; black marker pen; ruler; stapler; background paper fixed to the display area.

What to do
Encourage the children to use a pencil to draw around the jar template onto six sheets of A4 card. Help them to draw and cut out the same shape, six times, using a thick paper towel. Stick the six paper towel shapes onto the six card outlines. Cut out six brown paper 'beans' and stick them on to the paper towel shapes. Display all six pictures in a row. Label them 1 to 6.

Encourage the children to plant a bean in a jar and to watch it grow over a period of time (see the activity titled 'Roots and shoots' on page 36).

When the real bean begins to show a tiny root, help the children to decorate the second picture in the sequence with a simple sprouting root outline, drawn with felt-tipped pen on to the paper towel. The third picture will have the addition of a growing shoot coloured in green. The fourth picture will show the shoot as a green-coloured stem growing out of the jar and on to the paper above. (Remember that the root outline will also have grown longer and will have additional root hairs.) For the fifth picture, a child can cut out two green paper leaves and stick them onto the stalk above the neck of the jar. The final picture will have additional leaves and more root hairs (see illustration below).

DISCUSSION
Ask questions about this picture sequence to help the children with direction, left and right, space words, size and comparison. Questions might include: *What is happening in the picture to the left of number 2? Which picture comes after/ before number 5? What is on the first picture? Which picture has the tallest bean/the least amount of leaves/the biggest leaves/ the longest root?*

Daisy chain

What you need

Large piece of pale green backing paper to fit your display area; staple gun (adult use only); white and green card; circular templates in various sizes; real daisies or pictures of daisies; crayons; scissors; adhesive tape; pencils.

What to do

Encourage each child to draw round the circular template on to the white card and to cut it out. Ask the children to look at real daisies and ask them to identify the colour of the centre. Invite them to select a matching colour to decorate the centre of their circle. Observe the pink rim around the petals on the real daisies. Help the children to colour a pink 'rim' round the outer edge of their circle. Fold the circle in half and then half again with the coloured side on the outside and help the children to cut thin vertical strips from the pink outer edge up to the edge of the 'yellow' circle in the middle. Invite each child to cut a long 'stem' using green card and help them to write their first name on it, then use adhesive tape to attach the stem to the back of the daisy head in the centre. Make a vertical cut at the bottom end of each flower stem. Show the children how to thread their daisy at right angles into a friend's until all the daisies make a chain (as shown in the illustration). Flick some of the petals upwards and inwards on each daisy before stapling the chain on to the background paper. Label the diagram 'Our daisy chain of friends'.

DISCUSSION

A chain is a way of joining lots of separate (usually metal) pieces together, that still allows each piece or link to move. Can the children think of any uses for chains? (Bicycles, jewellery, hanging baskets.) How could the children make a chain of themselves? Show them how to link arms and let them sway from side to side as they sing a song together.

Our daisy chain of friends

Dingle, dangle scarecrow

Clive Barnwell

Dandelion clock

Jan Holdstock

Grandad loves his garden

Gran - dad loves his gar - den, you will find him ev - 'ry day,
Work - ing hard out in the yard and whist - l - ing a - way.

Chorus
Dig - ging and ra - king — siev - ing and sha - king, plant - ing the seeds — in a row,
Wat - er - ing weed - ing and spray - ing and feed - ing and watch - ing the gar - den grow.

2. Grandad says it keeps him fit
And out of mischief too
Whatever kind of weather
There are always things to do.

Chorus
Digging and raking...

Debbie Campbell

Our food

To the tune of 'Incy Wincy Spider'.

2. Sugar cane like to grow where it's hot and wet.
   It grows in Cuba and it grows in Brazil.

3. Rice like to grow where it's steamy and hot.
   It grows in China and it grows in Japan.

4. Lemons like to grow where it's warm and dry.
   They grow in Israel and they grow in Spain.

Sally Scott

Farmer, farmer

To the tune of 'London Bridge is falling down'.

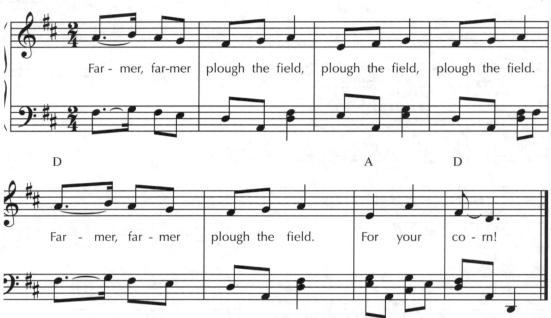

2. Farmer, Farmer rake it smooth
   For your corn!

3. Farmer, Farmer sow your corn
   Sow your corn!

4. Farmer, Farmer wait for rain
   To water your corn!

5. Farmer, Farmer watch the shoots
   Growing tall.

6. Farmer, Farmer cut the corn
   Cut the corn!

Sally Scott

Growing up

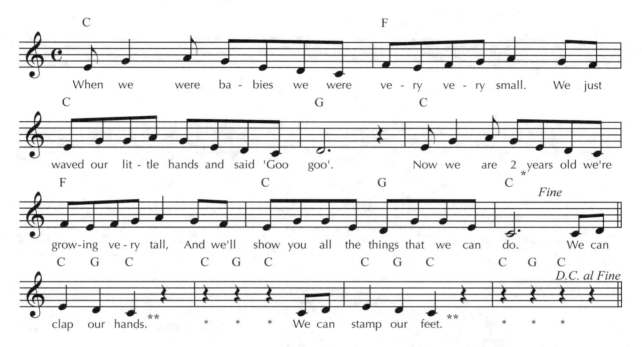

When we were ba-bies we were ve-ry ve-ry small. We just waved our lit-tle hands and said 'Goo goo'. Now we are 2 years old we're grow-ing ve-ry tall, And we'll show you all the things that we can do. We can clap our hands.** * * * We can stamp our feet.** * * *

Additional verses on CD-ROM

At * sing the children's age.
If some of the children are older than others,
sing a different age in each verse.

At ** insert two different actions in each verse.
The verses can be cumulative if you like.

If you are talking about babies, you may like to
replace 'waved our little hands' with other suitable
actions.

Jan Holdstock

The sunflower song

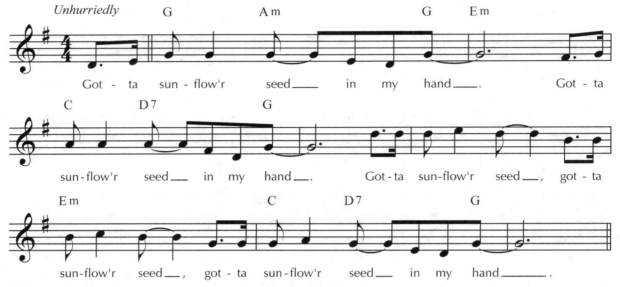

Unhurriedly

Got - ta sun - flow'r seed___ in my hand___. Got - ta

sun - flow'r seed___ in my hand___. Got - ta sun - flow'r seed___, got - ta

sun - flow'r seed___, got - ta sun - flow'r seed___ in my hand_____.

Sue Nicholls

Additional verses on CD-ROM

The three little pigs

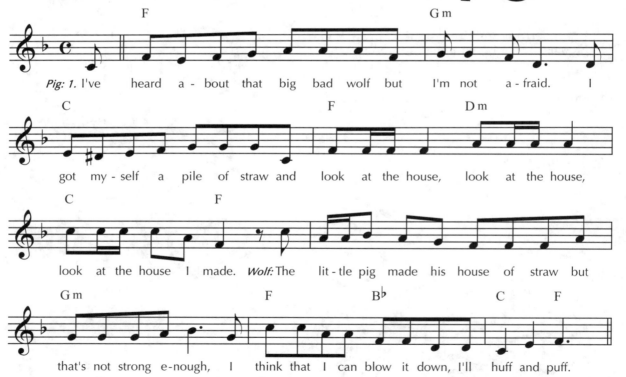

Pig: 1. I've heard a - bout that big bad wolf but I'm not a - fraid. I

got my - self a pile of straw and look at the house, look at the house,

look at the house I made. *Wolf:* The lit - tle pig made his house of straw but

that's not strong e - nough, I think that I can blow it down, I'll huff and puff.

Jan Holdstock

Additional verses on CD-ROM

A seed

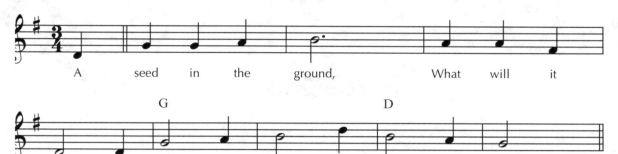

A seed in the ground, What will it

be, a ti - ny plant, Or gi - ant tree?

2. A seed on a tree,
   Where will it fall?
   On to the ground
   Or stuck on a wall?

3. Where will I go?
   The seed of a pea?
   Fall to the ground
   Or cooked for tea?

4. A seed that has wings,
   Where will it blow?
   Spinning around
   Then landing so.

5. A dandelion clock,
   Blowing around;
   This way and that
   Then down to the ground.

Carole Henderson-Begg

Caterpillar

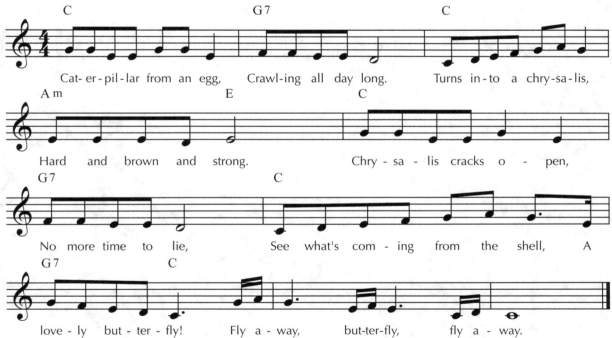

Cat- er - pil - lar from an egg, Crawl-ing all day long. Turns in-to a chry-sa-lis,

Hard and brown and strong. Chry - sa - lis cracks o - pen,

No more time to lie, See what's com - ing from the shell, A

love - ly but - ter - fly! Fly a - way, but-ter-fly, fly a - way.

Jean Gilbert

Tadpole

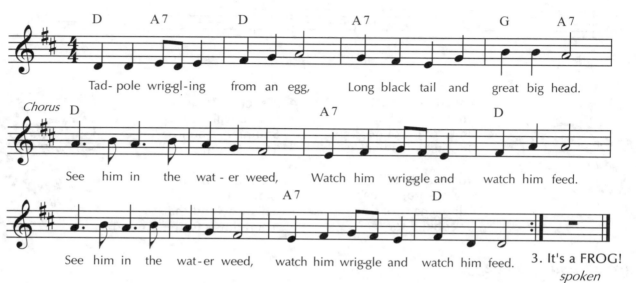

Tad-pole wrig-gl-ing from an egg, Long black tail and great big head.

Chorus

See him in the wat-er weed, Watch him wrig-gle and watch him feed.

See him in the wat-er weed, watch him wrig-gle and watch him feed.

3. It's a FROG!
spoken

2. Shrinking tail and growing limbs,
   Tadpole's changing as he swims.
   See him in the water-weed,
   Watch him wriggle and watch him feed.
   See him in the water-weed,
   Watch him wriggle and watch him feed.

3. Lost his tail but now he's found,
   Strong back legs to jump around.
   Jumping high into a bush,
   Jumping into the water, splash!
   Jumping high into a bush,
   Jumping into the water, splash!
   It's a FROG! (spoken)

Jean Gilbert

A seedy story

In the dark, dark earth
was a small, small seed.
And the sun came up
and the rain came down.

From the small, small seed
burst a white, white root.
And the sun came up
and the root pushed down.

From the small, small seed
crept a brave, brave shoot.
And the shoot grew up
and the rain came down.

From the damp, damp soil
crept the brave, brave shoot.
And the shoot grew green
and the sun shone down.

From the green, green shoot
grew a tall, tall tree.
And the sun came up
and the rain came down.

On the tall, tall tree
grew A PLUM for me!
And the sun came up
and the sun came down.

Judith Nicholls

Actions
The children can act out this poem in pairs.
Child 1 is the seed, starting curled up and
using one hand for the root, the other for
the shoot, gradually stretching higher and
stretching arms out. One hand can be used
to make a plum shape. Child 2 (or an adult)
is the sun and rain, using arms and hands for
appropriate actions – then picking the plum
at the end!
  The poem can be arranged as two-line
verses if preferred.

Daisy chain

Ten dancing daisies
Growing in a line
The wind blew one of them away
Then there were nine

Nine dancing daisies
By the garden gate
A hungry goat had one for lunch
Then there were eight

Eight dancing daisies
When along came Kevin
He took one home for his mum
Then there were seven

Seven dancing daisies
One got in a fix
She fell down and broke her stem
Then there were six

Six dancing daisies
In front of the beehive
A busy bee buzzed into one
Then there were five

Five dancing daisies
When the rain began to pour
One was washed out in the storm
Then there were four

Four dancing daisies
Happy as can be
A butterfly sat down on one
Then there were three

Three dancing daisies
Wondering what to do
I put one behind my ear
Then there were two

Two dancing daisies
Swaying in the sun
A bird used one to line her nest
Then there was one

One dancing daisy
Standing all alone
She went to join a daisy chain
Then there were none!

Fiona McGarry

Actions
Choose ten children to stand in the centre of the ring as the 'daisies'. Point to each daisy in turn to leave the daisy chain and return to join the rest of the group.
Verse 1: Blow one of the daisies away.
Verse 2: Munch as if eating a daisy.
Verse 3: Stoop as if to pick a flower.
Verse 4: Bend suddenly from the waist.
Verse 5: With forefinger and thumb together, imitate the flight of a bee landing on a flower.
Verse 6: Use hands and fingers to imitate rain falling.
Verse 7: Pretend to be a butterfly. Sit down.
Verse 8: Place one finger on chin as if wondering, then pretend to put a flower behind their ear.
Verse 9: Flap arms like birds wings.
Verse 10: All join hands to make one long chain.

When I was a baby

When I was a baby
I was small, small, small
Now that I am bigger
I am tall, tall, tall
I'm not as tall as Mummy, or Daddy,
or a tree
I'm really just the right size for me!

When I was a baby
I would sleep all day
Now that I am bigger
All I want to do is play
No cooking and no cleaning and no
driving the car
I like things just the way they are!

Jan Jones

Actions
Children mime stretching, curling actions,
and so on, as suggested in the poem.

Birthdays

Every year another candle
added to your birthday cake.
How old are you now, I wonder?
How many birthdays does that make?

Getting bigger, growing taller,
larger shoes to fit your feet,
every year we all grow older,
birthdays are a special treat.

Fun and games and happy faces
lots of presents from our friends,
every year we all have birthdays,
let's hope birthdays never end.

Jan Pollard

Apple, plum, peach, pear

Apple, plum, peach, pear
Trees in blossom everywhere.

Apple, pear, plum, peach
Clouds of blossom just in reach.

Apple, peach, pear, plum
Dressed in pink and white, each one.

Brenda Williams

The tadpole

Underneath the water-weeds
Small and black, I wriggle,
And life is most surprising!
Wiggle! waggle! wiggle!
There's every now and then a most
Exciting change in me,
I wonder, wiggle! waggle!
What I shall turn out to be!

Elizabeth Gould

Growing flowers

First we dig the soil,
Then we plant the seeds,
We water them regularly,
And pull up the weeds.

Soon some tiny shoots,
Push out of the ground,
Reaching for the sun,
Growing without a sound.

At last the buds appear,
Closed up all tight,
Slowly they open up,
Into a wonderful sight.

Karen King

Actions
The children stand in a line and
do the following actions.
Verse 1: The children pretend to
dig the soil, then plant the seeds,
water the garden, pull up some
weeds.
Verse 2: The children bend their
knees and crouch down, then
start standing up slowly, and
stretch their arms in the air.
Verse 3: The children half-cover
their faces with their hands then
slowly move their hands away
from their faces and stretch their
arms out wide, smiling.

Herbs for cooking

Mint, basil,
parsley, sage,

Herbs to use
in different ways.

Mint for potatoes,
new, of course.

Parsley for fish
in pure white sauce.

Basil for pasta,
tastes just right.

Sage for turkey,
on Christmas night.

Herbs for cooking
Lovely smell,

Herbs for taste
and health as well!

Brenda Williams

Planting trees

Here comes the lorry with small baby trees

Here comes the gardener with mud on his knees

Here comes the digger to dig a big ditch

Here comes the leaf mould to make the soil rich.

Plant the small trees deep in the ground

Throw in more soil and trample around.

Wait for the sunshine to make the trees grow

Wait for the spring when leaves start to show

Wait for the trees to grow tall and strong

Wait till the birds come to fill them with song.

Then in the summer on long summer days

Sit at its roots for a rest in the shade.

Brenda Williams

Actions

Mime driving a lorry

Walk heavily

Use two arms to scoop and lift

Mime throwing into ditch

Pretend to lift and carry trees

Throw, and stamp around

Throw arms up and out from
chest to indicate sunshine
Wriggle fingers

Stand tall and strong

Fly around

Throw arms up and out from
chest to indicate sunshine
Lie down and mime sleeping

Grown out of

My trousers are tight,
they just won't fit.

And my jumper?
I've grown out of it.

My shirt's too short,
it just won't do.

There are holes in my socks
where my toes push through.

It's lucky I don't grow out of my skin.
'Cos then there'd be *nothing*
to put me in!

Tony Mitton

The farmer knows

The farmer loves
the falling rain.
He knows it helps
to grow the grain.

The farmer loves
the shining sun.
It feeds his growing plants,
each one.

The farmer loves
the rich, brown earth.
He knows what soil
is really worth.

With these good things,
the farmer knows,
everything lives,
everything grows.

Tony Mitton

The crop song

This is the song
the seed sings:
sow, sow, sow.

This is the song
the shoot sings:
grow, grow, grow.

This is the song
the root sings:
deep, deep, deep.

And this is the song
the farmer sings:
reap, reap, reap.

Tony Mitton

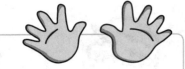

Actions
Sow seeds from a basket.

Slowly raise a hand upwards,
with twisty arm movement.

Point hand downwards and
lower arm slowly, to mimic
root.

Gather sheaves into arms, or
drive tractor.

Save our trees

Newspaper
Wrapping paper
Comic or book.

Paper all around us
Everywhere we look.

Kitchen paper
Writing paper
Catalogues and such.

Paper all around us
There is just so much!

Save paper
Use paper
Anyway you know.

Save our trees
And let them grow.

Brenda Williams

In this series:

ISBN 0-439-96559-4
ISBN 978-0439-96559-0

ISBN 0-439-96558-6
ISBN 978-0439-96558-3

ISBN 0-439-96560-8
ISBN 978-0439-96560-6

ISBN 0-439-96557-8
ISBN 978-0439-96557-6

To find out more about **Themes for Early Years** or to order additional copies
of the CD-ROMs call **0845 603 9091**

**New Themes for Early Years - available Spring 2007
Minibeasts ISBN 0-439-94497-X
People who help us ISBN 0-439-94498-8**

Visit our website **www.scholastic.co.uk**